WONDERS NEVER CEASE

Even if you think you've seen it all, get ready for some incredible surprises. The world is full of fantastic people, strange places, and bizarre things—and the tireless Ripley researchers keep on digging them up for your amusement and amazement.

If you cannot find your favorite *Believe It or Not!* POCKET BOOK at your local newsstand, please write to the nearest Ripley's "Believe It or Not!" museum:

P.O. Box 2394
Myrtle Beach, South Carolina 29577

175 Jefferson Street, San Francisco,
California 94133

1500 North Wells Street, Chicago,
Illinois 60610

19 San Marco Avenue, St. Augustine,
Florida 32084

Rebel Corners, Gatlinburg,
Tennessee 37738

145 East Elkhorn Avenue, Estes Park,
Colorado 80517

4960 Clifton Hill, Niagara Falls,
Canada L2G 3N5

Central Promenade, Blackpool
Lancashire, England FY1 5AA

Ripley's Believe It or Not! titles

Ripley's Believe It or Not! 2nd Series
Ripley's Believe It or Not! 3rd Series
Ripley's Believe It or Not! 4th Series
Ripley's Believe It or Not! 5th Series
Ripley's Believe It or Not! 6th Series
Ripley's Believe It or Not! 7th Series
Ripley's Believe It or Not! 8th Series
Ripley's Believe It or Not! 9th Series
Ripley's Believe It or Not! 10th Series
Ripley's Believe It or Not! 11th Series
Ripley's Believe It or Not! 12th Series
Ripley's Believe It or Not! 13th Series
Ripley's Believe It or Not! 14th Series
Ripley's Believe It or Not! 15th Series
Ripley's Believe It or Not! 16th Series
Ripley's Believe It or Not! 17th Series
Ripley's Believe It or Not! 18th Series
Ripley's Believe It or Not! 19th Series
Ripley's Believe It or Not! 20th Series
Ripley's Believe It or Not! 21st Series
Ripley's Believe It or Not! 22nd Series
Ripley's Believe It or Not! 23rd Series
Ripley's Believe It or Not! 24th Series
Ripley's Believe It or Not! 25th Series
Ripley's Believe It or Not! 26th Series
Ripley's Believe It or Not! 27th Series
Ripley's Believe It or Not! Anniversary Edition
Ripley's Believe It or Not! Book of Americana
Ripley's Believe It or Not! Book of the Military
Ripley's Believe It or Not! Book of Undersea Oddities
Ripley's Believe It or Not! Tombstones and Graveyards

Published by POCKET BOOKS

Ripley's Believe It or Not!

27th Series

A KANGAROO BOOK

PUBLISHED BY POCKET BOOKS NEW YORK

RIPLEY'S BELIEVE IT OR NOT!® 27th SERIES

POCKET BOOK edition published November, 1977

This original POCKET BOOK edition is printed from brand-new plates. POCKET BOOK editions are published by
POCKET BOOKS,
a Simon & Schuster Division of
GULF & WESTERN CORPORATION
1230 Avenue of the Americas,
New York, N.Y. 10020.
Trademarks registered in the United States
and other countries.

PREFACE

As fans of *Ripley's Believe It Or Not* know, Robert Ripley traveled extensively during his lifetime and accumulated an assortment of curious memorabilia and knowledge of unusual phenomena for later use in his worldwide syndicated newspaper feature and his radio and television shows. But we wonder if all our fans are aware of the great variety of curiosities, exhibits, and incredible facts that can be personally viewed today by the avid Ripley fan. Yes, Ripley's has eight Believe It Or Not Museums, each presenting the fascinating world of Ripley.

Shortly after Mr. Ripley's death in 1949, the first permanent Ripley Museum was established in St. Augustine, Florida, the nation's oldest city. People flocked from miles around to visit this unusual and unique showplace.

However, it was not until 1959 that the second full-scale permanent Ripley Museum was opened in Niagara Falls, Canada. Fisherman's Wharf, San Francisco, boasted a Ripley Museum in 1966, followed in 1968 by Chicago's Old Town.

The Great Smoky Mountains National Park, in Tennessee, is visited annually by more tourists than any other National Park in the United States, so what more fitting place for a Ripley Museum than Gatlinburg, the town nestled in the heart of the Smokies. It's been a favorite since its 1970 opening.

The fascination of Ripley's, of course, is worldwide, and in 1971, a Ripley Odditorium was opened in Blackpool, England. "Odditorium" was a name Robert Ripley himself coined, and to our knowledge no other museum in England had adopted this unusual title; perfect for Ripley's.

Seventy-five hundred feet up in the Rocky Mountains, in Estes Park, Colorado, a Ripley Museum opened in 1973. The latest and largest Ripley Museum opened amid great fanfare in Myrtle Beach, South Carolina on Bicentennial Weekend, 1976.

All Ripley Museums house actual items collected by Robert Ripley on his travels. Many of his famous cartoons are recreated in actual scenes. New and unbelievable facts have been unearthed and displayed, giving the visitor as much pleasure as our Pocket Books have brought countless readers over the years. We hope you continue to enjoy our books and visit, and re-visit, our museums.

Ripley International Limited,
Toronto, Ontario, Canada.

Ripley's ·Believe It or Not!

27th Series

THE **BELFRY** OF THE CHURCH OF ST. PANKRATIUS IN Iserlohn, Germany, **197 FEET HIGH,** IS THE TOWN'S OLDEST STRUCTURE -- *BUILT 400 YEARS BEFORE THE CHURCH ITSELF*

JOHN ROSS (1790-1866) A CHIEF OF THE AMERICAN CHEROKEE INDIANS, WAS ONLY *ONE-QUARTER CHEROKEE.* HIS FATHER WAS SCOTCH AND HIS MOTHER WAS ONE-QUARTER CHEROKEE AND 3/4 SCOTCH

A **GROUND SQUIRREL** BY BOOSTING THE HEAT PRODUCTION OF ITS FAT, IN 3 HOURS CAN RAISE ITS BODY TEMPERATURE 30 DEGREES C.

THE **STRANGEST "NECKLACES"** IN THE WORLD **MEN** OF THE SHILLUK TRIBE OF THE SUDAN, AFRICA, AS THEIR INITIATION INTO ADULTHOOD, ORNAMENT THEIR FOREHEADS WITH A "STRING OF BEADS" -- *CREATED BY FILLING INCISIONS WITH GUNPOWDER*

9

HOW THE ABORIGINES COPE WITH THE HIGH COST OF SUGAR

THE MANNA GUM TREE of Australia, HAS SUGARY SCALES CREATED BY A TINY INSECT, *WHICH ABORIGINES COLLECT AS SWEETENERS*

THE JACKFRUIT of the Philippines, WEIGHS AS MUCH *AS 80 POUNDS*

A **LIZARD** SMELLS THROUGH ITS FORKED TONGUE

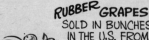

RUBBER GRAPES SOLD IN BUNCHES IN THE U.S. FROM 1887 TO 1920, WERE WORN BY LADIES AND USED AS TABLE DECORATIONS--WITH EACH GRAPE CONTAINING *BRANDY, WHISKEY, GIN OR WINE*

THE **GEOGRAPHICAL CONE** SO NAMED BECAUSE IT BEARS A MAP-LIKE DESIGN-- HAS A POISONOUS STING *THAT CAN KILL A MAN*

THE **HAIRDO** OF A JAPANESE GEISHA CAN REQUIRE 12 HOURS OF LABOR TO COMPLETE--EMBRACING ARTIFICIAL FLOWERS AND METAL BUTTERFLIES **WHICH FLUTTER THEIR WINGS WHEN SHE BOWS**

THE **TOWER** OF THE MUNICIPAL LIBRARY IN Copenhagen, Denmark, WAS ORIGINALLY THE BELFRY OF THE NICOLAI CHURCH *WHICH WAS DESTROYED, EXCEPT FOR THE TOWER -- IN 1795*

THE **FIRST MOTION PICTURE STUDIO** CREATED BY THOMAS ALVA EDISON IN EAST ORANGE, N.J., IN 1893, WAS MOUNTED ON A PIVOT SO ITS STAGE COULD BE TURNED TO THE SUN-- *AND COST $637*

DRESS BOOTS WORN BY ROMAN ARMY OFFICERS, OFTEN WERE ADORNED WITH *THE PAWS AND HEAD OF A SMALL ANIMAL*

11

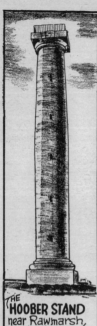

THE HOOBER STAND near Rawmarsh, England, WAS BUILT HIGH ENOUGH TO OVERLOOK EXACTLY **50 CHURCHES AND 50 COAL MINES**

MRS. ANNE DISRAELI WIFE OF BRITISH PREMIER BENJAMIN DISRAELI, WAS MADE A PEERESS IN HER OWN RIGHT IN 1868, AT HER FAMOUS HUSBAND'S REQUEST -- *BECAUSE HE WANTED HER TO OUTRANK HIM.* NOT UNTIL 4 YEARS AFTER HER DEATH DID DISRAELI CONSENT TO BECOME A LORD

THE WELL OF DOON Donegal, Ireland, IS SURROUNDED WITH BANDAGES AND CRUTCHES, ABANDONED BY VISITORS CONVINCED THAT THEY WERE CURED *MERELY BY DRINKING ITS WATERS*

A COFFIN FOUND IN Massarah, Egypt, IN 1888, WAS MADE FROM THE ENTIRE HIDE OF A CROCODILE

OPTICAL ILLUSION IS THE MAN LOOKING DOWN -- OR AT THE CARD HE IS HOLDING?

A **SAWMILL** IN HAARLEM, THE NETHERLANDS, SO BUILT THAT THE ENTIRE STRUCTURE TURNS *TO FACE THE WIND*

EMPEROR WU TI WHO RULED CHINA FOR 47 YEARS UNTIL 449, LEFT HIS THRONE 3 TIMES TO BECOME A BUDDHIST MONK -- *TWICE HE WAS PERSUADED TO RETURN TO THE THRONE, BUT THE THIRD TIME HE DECLINED AND HE DIED A MONK*

Crown Prince William (1781-1864) of Württemberg, TO AVOID MARRYING ONE OF NAPOLEON'S SISTERS, WAS MARRIED TO PRINCESS CHARLOTTE OF BAVARIA, BY PROXY-AND THEY NEVER MET ALTHOUGH THEY WERE *HUSBAND AND WIFE FOR 6 YEARS*

THE PRINCE WHO NEVER SAW HIS WIFE

THE **COLUMNAR PINE** GROWS ONLY IN ONE PLACE -- *THE ISLAND OF NEW CALEDONIA*

ANTO HIPONMA OF ʈᴇ ʜ CTORBDVN HOME JANVARI 1600 o P ANT·HIPPONMA OF Fʈ DRAGON 2·8 DECEMBER 1607

POST STONES LOCATED NEAR TABLE BAY, IN THE CAPE PROVINCE, SO. AFRICA, SERVED AS POST OFFICES FOR SHIP COMMANDERS **WHO LEFT LETTERS FOR EACH OTHER BENEATH THE STONES**

THE FIRST BEARDED LADIES **EGYPTIAN MONARCHS** FEMALE AS WELL AS MALE, WORE *FALSE BEARDS MADE OF GOLD OR OTHER METAL 5,000 YEARS AGO*

THE **ORNATE IRON RAILING** ON THE STAIRWAY IN THE CITY HALL OF NANCY, FRANCE, WAS FORGED IN A SINGLE OPERATION-- *YET, IT IS 82 FEET LONG*

THE **PYRAMID** of **ICHANG**, China, 500 FT. HIGH, AND ALMOST IDENTICAL TO EGYPT'S PYRAMID OF CHEOPS, *WAS CREATED OF SANDSTONE BY NATURE*

CARD-BOARD DISKS WERE USED AS MONEY IN DUTCH GUIANA IN 1820. *THE LARGER THE DISK, THE GREATER ITS VALUE*

MALISORI GIRLS of Albania, WEAR A BLACK SKIRT WITH WHITE STRIPES, AS A SIGNAL THAT *THEY ARE SINGLE*

STONES ON MOERAKI BEACH, NEAR DUNEDIN, SOUTH ISLAND, N.Z., *LOOK LIKE SUNNING TURTLES*

15

A **SEQUOIA LOG**
FOUND IMBEDDED IN SOFT
ROCK 30 FEET BELOW THE
SURFACE IN PLUMAS COUNTY,
CALIF., IS 10,000,000
YEARS OLD -- *YET IT IS
SO WELL PRESERVED
THAT IT WILL
STILL BURN*
Submitted by
Emery F. Tobin,
Vancouver, Wash.

TIBETAN HERDSMEN
WIELD SLINGSHOTS OF
HORSEHAIR AND WOOL
*THAT CAN KILL AT A
DISTANCE OF 150 FEET*

FINNISH STUDENTS
ARE PERMITTED TO WEAR
A WHITE CAP
*ONLY AFTER THEY HAVE
GRADUATED FROM HIGH
SCHOOL*

The SIDEWALK
in front of Holyrood Abbey, in Edinburgh, Scotland,
FOR CENTURIES WAS A SANCTUARY UPON WHICH *NO DEBTOR OR CRIMINAL COULD BE SEIZED*

A **FEMALE MAGPIE**
WHOSE MATE HAS DIED, IS COURTED IMMEDIATELY BY OTHER MALES WHO ASSEMBLE PROMPTLY NEAR THE DEAD MAGPIE'S BODY

KING NARATHIHAPATE
of Burma,
NEVER SNEEZED OR YAWNED *--AND ANYONE WHO DID EITHER IN HIS PRESENCE WAS BEHEADED* (1255-1290)

A **BUTTERFLY** THAT FRIGHTENS AWAY ITS ENEMIES BY A CAMOUFLAGE DESIGN, MAKING IT LOOK *LIKE AN OWL*

A **CHARM**
WHICH THE AZANDE OF AFRICA BLOW, IN THE BELIEF IT WILL MAKE THE WHISTLER *INVISIBLE*

JUDGE ABRAHAM FULLER (1720-1794) of Newton, Mass., WAS SO FANATICALLY OPPOSED TO DEBTS THAT WHEN A PHYSICIAN WAS CALLED TO WRITE OUT HIS DEATH CERTIFICATE, THE DOCTOR FOUND HIS FEE *IN THE DEAD MAN'S CLENCHED FIST*

THE **BASILICA** OF **ST. CLEMENT** IN ROME, ITALY, WAS BUILT IN THE 12th CENTURY OVER AN OLDER CHURCH ERECTED IN THE 4th CENTURY-- *WHICH RESTED ON THE RUINS OF A PAGAN TEMPLE*

THE **TAMILS** of India, DRINK WATER BY POURING IT INTO THEIR MOUTHS *BECAUSE THEY ARE FORBIDDEN TO TOUCH THE WATER VESSEL TO THEIR LIPS*

18

THE BUILDING THAT WAS ERECTED TO QUELL A RUMOR

THE ABBEY OF BURTON in Staffordshire, England, WAS CONSTRUCTED SOLELY TO REASSURE THE POPULACE *THE WORLD WAS NOT GOING TO END IN THE YEAR 1,000*

A *YOUNG* MAN IN THE BHAMTA TRIBE, INDIA, CANNOT MARRY UNTIL HE HAS BEEN *ARRESTED AT LEAST 14 TIMES*

THE LARVA OF THE GOLDEN EYES INSECT CAMOUFLAGES ITSELF BY COVERING ITS BACK *WITH TRASH*

THE MALE MASKED WEAVER OF SOUTH AFRICA, WHICH IS POLYGAMOUS, BUILDS SEVERAL NESTS-- *ONE FOR EACH MATE*

THE SMOKING PIPES OF THE ALEUTS, OF THE ALEUTIAN ISLANDS, ARE OFTEN CARVED IN THE LIKE-NESS OF THE SMOKER

NATIVES OF THE CONGO, PERFORM A DANCE WITH ARROWS PIERCING THEIR CHEEKS--*TO HONOR THE ANCESTOR TO WHOM THE ARROWS ONCE BELONGED*

THE STATE BEDROOM IN HERRENCHIEMSEE CASTLE, BAVARIA, *HAS NEVER BEEN SLEPT IN.* THE BAVARIAN KING WHO BUILT THE CASTLE IN 1883 STIPULATED THIS BEDROOM WAS ONLY FOR SHOW

A **CHALICE** GIVEN TO POTEMKIN BY CATHERINE THE GREAT, OF RUSSIA, *CONTAINS 1,300 DIAMONDS*

PEPPERED MOTHS of England HAVE ESCAPED DECIMATION BY PREDATORY BIRDS BECAUSE THEIR NORMAL WHITE COLOR HAS BECOME DARK IN RECENT YEARS --*ENABLING THEM TO BLEND INTO FOLIAGE DARKENED BY INDUSTRIAL POLLUTION*

ALL **SNAILS** ARE BISEXUAL

3,200 YEARS- *AND STILL NOT BALD!* PHARAOH RAMESES II (1292-1225 B.C.) OF EGYPT, WHEN HIS MUMMIFIED BODY WAS EXCAVATED, HAD RETAINED HIS HAIR FOR 3,200 YEARS

THE **CHURCH OF THE MADONNA OF THE SNOW** in Bevagna, Italy, WAS BUILT AS A *ROMAN TEMPLE 1,800 YEARS AGO*

AN **AMMONITE** THE COILED FOSSIL SHELL OF AN EXTINCT MOLLUSK, FOUND IN 1895, AND NOW IN THE STATE MUSEUM IN MUNSTER, GERMANY, *WEIGHS* **8,000 LBS.**

SKIN CREAM IN A COSMETICS JAR, FOUND IN KING TUT'S TOMB, WAS STILL IN GOOD CONDITION *AFTER 3,000 YEARS*

A **WATCH** OWNED BY MARY QUEEN OF SCOTS. MADE IN THE SHAPE OF A *HUMAN SKULL*

THE **ENTRANCE** TO AN ESTATE IN PEI HEI, CHINA, IS SHAPED LIKE A **CHINESE VASE**

Luca Antonio Pagnini
(1737 – 1814)

ITALIAN POET AND LINGUIST, FOR THE LAST 60 YEARS OF HIS LIFE SPENT AT LEAST *2 HOURS EACH DAY READING GREEK OR LATIN*

LOVE BIRDS CARRY BUILDING MATERIAL FOR THEIR NEST IN THE *FEATHERS ON THEIR BACK*

PRAIRIE DOGS IDENTIFY EACH OTHER BY "KISSING." *EACH PRESSES ITS TEETH AGAINST THE OTHER'S FACE*

OXEN IN FRANCE AND SPAIN, ARE BLINDFOLDED BY BASQUE FARMERS TO PROTECT *THEIR EYES FROM FLIES*

THE TOMBSTONE OF DAVID ANDRIST, SWISS ARCHEOLOGIST, IS AN ANCIENT ROCK HE DISCOVERED *AND BATTLED TO PROVE IT WAS BROUGHT TO THE AREA BY A GLACIER MILLIONS OF YEARS AGO*

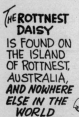

THE **MANED WOLF** of South America, HAS LEGS SO LONG, IT IS CALLED *"THE WOLF THAT WALKS ON STILTS"*

CHAUNCEY OLCOTT ONE OF THE MOST FAMOUS IRISH TENORS OF ALL TIME, *NEVER SAW IRELAND*

THE **ROTTNEST DAISY** IS FOUND ON THE ISLAND OF ROTTNEST, AUSTRALIA, *AND NOWHERE ELSE IN THE WORLD*

RUINS NEAR TEGHAZZA IN THE SAHARA DESERT, ARE THE REMAINS OF HOMES *BUILT OF PURE SALT*

NATURAL STONE BRIDGE OVER THE LEBEN RIVER, IN LEBANON

ANCIENT EGYPTIANS ALWAYS SHAVED OFF THEIR HAIR AS A RULE OF HYGIENE, AND A DOCTOR BASED HIS PATIENT'S FEE ON THE *WEIGHT OF THE HAIR SHAVED FROM A BEDRIDDEN PATIENT UPON HIS RECOVERY*

THE **OLDEST NATIONAL FLAG** THE WHITE CROSS OF DENMARK HAS BEEN USED FOR MORE THAN **700 YEARS**

URNS in the Marriage Chapel of the Hapsburgs in Vienna, Austria, PRESERVE THE HEARTS OF 54 MEMBERS OF THE IMPERIAL FAMILY, *EACH OF WHOM WAS MARRIED IN THE CHAPEL*

A **10-GULDEN BANKNOTE** ISSUED IN BADEN, GERMANY, IN 1849--AS A PROTECTION AGAINST COUNTERFEITING HAD ITS FACE DESIGN REPEATED ON ITS BACK, BUT PRINTED *IN REVERSE*

THE OLD SOLDIER
SERG. DONALD MACLEOD (1688-1791) of Skye, Scotland, SERVED IN THE BRITISH ARMY FOR 74 YEARS --*RETIRING AT THE AGE OF 88!* HE SERVED UNDER GEN. HENRY CLINTON IN THE ATTACK ON N.Y. WHEN HE WAS 87, AND WHEN HE DIED AT 103, HIS OLDEST SON WAS 84 AND HIS YOUNGEST WAS 10

THE **DRINKING MONSTER** HUNAFJORD, ICELAND, *NATURAL STONE FORMATION*

GOLD CIRCLETS WERE USED BY THE VIKINGS *AS MONEY*

THE **TIDE-POOL SHRIMP** IS SO TRANSPARENT THAT FOOD CAN BE SEEN PASSING FROM ITS MOUTH TO ITS STOMACH

BIRTHDAY EGG AN EGG LAID BY A CHICKEN OWNED BY JAY WEEMS, OF BATTLE GROUND, WASH., ON HIS BIRTHDAY, WAS EMBOSSED WITH *THE INITIAL "J"* Submitted by Emery F. Tobin, Vancouver, Wash.

THE PIGGYBACK CHURCH
THE CHURCH OF ST. FERMO
IN VERONA, ITALY, STANDS ATOP
A SUBTERRANEAN CHURCH
-AND SEPARATE SERVICES ARE
HELD IN EACH EDIFICE

EMPRESS BIANCA MARIA
OF GERMANY,
WAS FIRST ENGAGED AT
THE AGE OF 2 AND WAS BETROTHED
TO 6 DIFFERENT SUITORS
BEFORE SHE FINALLY
MARRIED EMPEROR
MAXIMILIAN OF GERMANY

VIA dell'AMORE
(THE WAY OF LOVE)
A PATH CARVED OUT OF A
ROCKY CLIFF OVER THE SEA
NEAR RIOMAGGIORE, ITALY,
WAS NAMED FOR THE ENGINEER
WHO DESIGNED IT, AMORE--
BUT IT IS NOW MUCH USED
AS A LOVERS' LANE

THE **CHURCH** of **ST. CATHERINE**
BUILT IN FROHNLEITEN, AUSTRIA,
IN THE 16th CENTURY, HAS
BEEN USED FOR 187 YEARS
AS AN APARTMENT HOUSE

THE **CONSUMMATE POLITICIAN**
Benjamin Disraeli BECAME
LEADER OF ENGLAND'S TORY
PARTY AND PRIME MINISTER
UNDER QUEEN VICTORIA AL-
THOUGH HE HAD SHOCKED
CONSERVATIVES BY PRODIGIOUS
PERSONAL DEBTS, FLASHY
DRESS, FLIGHTY LITERARY
WORKS, AND **3 LOSING
CAMPAIGNS AS A RADICAL.**

LAKE BENIT
IN SAVOY, FRANCE, IS
IN THE SHAPE OF A
GIANT FOOTPRINT

A **SINGLE
SILKWORM
COCOON**
CAN YIELD
*3,000 YARDS
OF SILK THREAD*

SYLVESTER GRAHAM

A PENNSYLVANIA PREACHER AFTER WHOM THE GRAHAM CRACKER WAS NAMED, WAS CONVINCED THAT A CRAVING FOR WHISKEY COULD BE CURED *BY EATING BREAD BAKED WITH BRAN*

THE **NYATPOLA PAGODA** IN Bhatgaon, Nepal, THE TALLEST IN THE COUNTRY, WAS BUILT IN 1703, IN 5 DAYS, AFTER KING BHUPATINDRA MALLA SET AN EXAMPLE BY *PERSONALLY CARRYING 3 BUILDING BLOCKS TO THE SITE*

THE **JAPANESE SYMBOL** FOR "MOUTH" 口 PLACED INSIDE THE SYMBOL FOR "GATE" 門

問

MEANS: "TO GET INFORMATION"

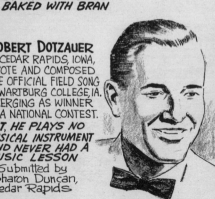

ROBERT DOTZAUER

OF CEDAR RAPIDS, IOWA, WROTE AND COMPOSED THE OFFICIAL FIELD SONG OF WARTBURG COLLEGE, IA. EMERGING AS WINNER IN A NATIONAL CONTEST. *YET, HE PLAYS NO MUSICAL INSTRUMENT AND NEVER HAD A MUSIC LESSON*

Submitted by Sharon Duncan, Cedar Rapids

28

THE **STATUE** WELCOMING VISITORS TO WAWA, ONTARIO, *IS A STEEL CANADIAN GOOSE 24 FT. HIGH AND WEIGHING 3,500 POUNDS.* WAWA IS THE INDIAN WORD FOR A CANADIAN GOOSE

Dorothy Catherine **DRAPER** THE SUBJECT OF A DAGUERREOTYPE MADE BY HER FATHER IN 1840, WAS THE FIRST PERSON EVER PHOTOGRAPHED WITH *THE MODEL'S EYES OPEN*

THE **CATHEDRAL** Pioche, Nevada, *NATURAL ROCK FORMATION*

A **MONKEY'S SKULL** STUFFED WITH COTTON, IS DISPLAYED OUTSIDE HOMES IN THE LUSHAI HILLS OF BURMA *TO FRIGHTEN AWAY STRANGERS*

THE **FLAG** OF THE FIRST TROOP, PHILADELPHIA CITY CAVALRY, WAS THE FIRST AMERICAN BANNER TO DISPLAY **13 STRIPES** (1775)

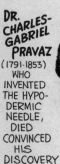

DR. **CHARLES-GABRIEL PRAVAZ** (1791-1853) WHO INVENTED THE HYPODERMIC NEEDLE, DIED CONVINCED HIS DISCOVERY *WAS A HOPELESS FAILURE*

THE CHAPEL OF THE SLIPPERS IN CEROUX-MOUSTY, BELGIUM, IS LINED WITH SLIPPERS HUNG BY GIRLS WHO BELIEVE *THIS WILL WIN THEM A HUSBAND*

THE CHURCH OF ST. MARY in Bressanoro, Italy, WAS BUILT BY EMPRESS BIANCA MARIA, OF GERMANY, AS A PENANCE BECAUSE SHE FAILED TO HONOR HER VOW *TO MAKE A PILGRIMAGE TO A SANCTUARY IN SPAIN*

THE BROOKLYN BRIDGE
THE NATION'S FIRST SUSPENSION BRIDGE BUILT WITH WIRE CABLES, CONTAINS IN THOSE CABLES MORE THAN 200 TONS OF DEFECTIVE STEEL--AND ITS NEW YORK TOWER RESTS ON SAND

A **GRAND-MOTHER'S CLOCK** NATIONAL MUSEUM, HELSINKI, FINLAND,

SHAPED LIKE A **WOMAN**

JEAN CAVALIER
(1681-1740)
A FRENCH BAKER, AS A SOLDIER FOUGHT FOR FRANCE, ITALY, HOLLAND AND BRITAIN--*AND IN 1738 BECAME A MAJOR GENERAL IN THE BRITISH ARMY*

THE ENGAGEMENT RING OF A GIRL OF THE NGOMNE TRIBE, AFRICA, IS A WIRE SPIRAL SHE WEARS ON HER ANKLE

A **HUGE BANYAN TREE** IN THE MARQUESAS ISLANDS, IN THE PACIFIC, SERVED AS A *TRIBAL CEMETERY*

ANNIE SMITH PECK FIRST AMERICAN WOMAN TO CLIMB THE MATTERHORN, *WAS AN ACTIVE ALPINIST UNTIL SHE WAS 82*

Winter Magdalen Mail

A CASK OF MAIL DROPPED INTO THE ST. LAWRENCE RIVER IN 1910 BY NATIVES OF THE MAGDALEN ISLANDS, QUEBEC, INDUCED THE CANADIAN GOVERNMENT TO GIVE THE ISLANDS *A WIRELESS LINK WITH THE OUTSIDE WORLD*

JAMES TYSON
AUSTRALIA'S FIRST CATTLE KING, LEFT AN ESTATE OF MORE THAN $6,000,000 IN 1898, BUT HE HAD MADE NO WILL BECAUSE HE DISLIKED *ALL HIS RELATIVES WITH EQUAL INTENSITY*

THE
PRINCE de CONDÉ
LED A REVOLT AGAINST KING LOUIS XIV of France, in 1652, BUT THE MONARCH RESTORED HIM TO HONOR-- EXPLAINING THAT A MAN OF SUCH GREAT MILITARY TALENT WOULD BE *LESS DANGEROUS AS A FRIEND THAN AS A FOE*

THE **HOME** of THOMAS NELSON at Yorktown, Va., STILL HAS IN ITS WALLS THE CANNON BALLS ORDERED FIRED BY ITS OWNER IN 1781, BECAUSE BRITISH GEN. CORNWALLIS HAD SEIZED IT FOR HIS HEADQUARTERS

THE CHURCH OF CURTEA de ARGESH IN ARGESH, RUMANIA, WAS COMPLETED IN 1508 --AND ON THE DAY OF ITS COMPLETION THE ARCHITECT, MANOLE, *LEAPED TO HIS DEATH FROM ITS ROOF*

BLANCHE KELSO BRUCE WHO SERVED IN THE MISSISSIPPI STATE SENATE FROM 1875 UNTIL 1881, *WAS AN ESCAPED SLAVE*

THE STATE BARGE USED BY THE KINGS OF OUDH, INDIA, IS SHAPED LIKE THE ROYAL FAMILY'S EMBLEM -- *A FISH*

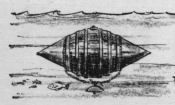

CHAINS OF "TORPEDOES" WERE MOORED IN HARBORS IN THE CIVIL WAR BY THE CONFEDERATES *WHO MADE THEM FROM BEER BARRELS LOADED WITH GUNPOWDER*

THE SPAN OVER A RIVER NEAR AGADIR, MOROCCO, WAS MADE FROM THE *BARK OF A SINGLE GIANT TREE*

PARLIAMENT SQUARE in Edinburgh, Scotland, FEATURES A HEART DESIGN IN ITS PAVEMENT--SYMBOLIZING *THE CITY'S POETIC NAME* "THE HEART OF MIDLOTHIAN"

THE **BAPTISMAL FONT** OF ST. PRISCA'S CHURCH, IN ROME, ITALY, ORIGINALLY WAS THE CAP OF A COLUMN *IN A PAGAN TEMPLE*

Thomas **TELFORD** (1757-1834) FAMED SCOTTISH ENGINEER, CONSTRUCTED 920 MILES OF ROADS AND **1,200 BRIDGES**

ONE TOWN
WOMEN'S LIBBERS
HAVE OVERLOOKED
KARYES, ON THE PENIN-
SULA OF MT. ATHOS, GREECE,
IN ACCORDANCE WITH A
CONSTITUTION WRITTEN
IN 1045, BARS ALL
FEMALES AT ITS GATES-
EVEN FEMALE ANIMALS

A **DRAWING** OF AN INDIAN OXCART
DRIVER WHOSE NOSE WAS
CUT OFF BY A CRUEL RULER AND
REPLACED ARTIFICIALLY IN 1794,
INSPIRED AN ENGLISH SURGEON,
DR. JOSEPH C. CARPUE, TO CREATE
A WAX NOSE FOR LIEUT. CHARLES
TURNER, 20 YEARS LATER

THE **SEA COW**
A FISH--HAS HORNS
AND LARGE EYES LIKE
THOSE OF A COW

THE MONSTRANCE
IN THE CATHEDRAL TREASURY
OF SALZBURG, AUSTRIA, IS
STUDDED WITH 1,792 DIAMONDS,
24 EMERALDS, 405 RUBIES
AND 16 SAPPHIRES

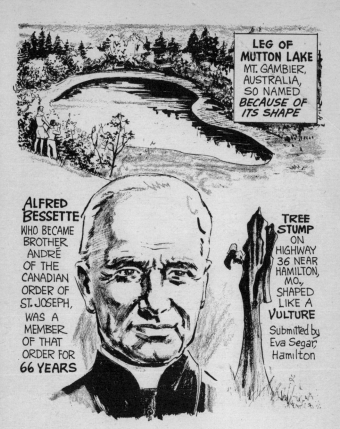

LEG OF MUTTON LAKE MT. GAMBIER, AUSTRALIA, SO NAMED *BECAUSE OF ITS SHAPE*

ALFRED BESSETTE WHO BECAME BROTHER ANDRÉ OF THE CANADIAN ORDER OF ST. JOSEPH, WAS A MEMBER OF THAT ORDER FOR **66 YEARS**

TREE STUMP ON HIGHWAY 36 NEAR HAMILTON, MO, SHAPED LIKE A **VULTURE**

Submitted by Eva Segar, Hamilton

THE JONATHAN FAIRBANKS HOUSE of Dedham, Mass, BUILT IN 1636, *IS THE OLDEST FRAME HOUSE IN AMERICA*

THE ARM and TORCH
OF THE STATUE OF LIBERTY WERE RUSHED TO COMPLETION IN FRANCE IN 1876 FOR *EXHIBIT IN PHILADELPHIA AT THE CENTENNIAL FAIR*

CALF
BORN WITH 5 LEGS
Submitted by R.W. Johnson
Lynchburg, Va.

JAPANESE BRIDES
WEAR WHITE PAPER HATS
TO ASSURE MARITAL FIDELITY AND AN ABSENCE OF JEALOUSY

BUSHMEN
OF AFRICA, DRINK SOUP BY MEANS OF A BRUSH MADE FROM THE BACK HAIR OF A HYENA

THE GREAT GUN of TANJORE - India -
27 FT. LONG AND 2½ FT. IN DIAMETER, WAS FIRED ONCE IN 400 YEARS.
THE GUNNER LIT A GUNPOWDER "FUSE" FROM A SPOT ONE MILE AWAY

UGGUCION DELLA FAGGIOLA
(1250-1319) AN ITALIAN MERCENARY,
OWNED 72 CASTLES -- AND
THROUGHOUT HIS ADULT LIFE,
*SLEPT AT LEAST TWICE EACH
YEAR IN EVERY ONE OF THEM*

PETER TOTH
AN ARTIST SPECIALIZING IN
SCULPTURES OF AMERICAN
INDIANS, **HAS DONATED
HIS CARVINGS, MANY OF
THEM 20 FT. HIGH, TO
PARKS IN 11 STATES**
Submitted by Emery F. Tobin,
Vancouver, Washington

THE **TOWERS** OF THE
CHURCH OF TOUCY,
France,
ORIGINALLY WERE PART
OF THE ANCIENT CITY
WALL--MOST OF
*WHICH WAS
DESTROYED
552 YEARS AGO*

BASKETS
MADE BY
**AFRICAN
TRIBESMEN
FROM PORCU-
PINE QUILLS**

A TURKISH CANNON
LEFT ON A REMNANT OF THE WALLS OF BASRA IN IRAQ, WHEN THE TURKS WERE OUSTED FROM THE CITY IN WORLD WAR I, *HAS BECOME A NATIONAL MONUMENT AT WHICH MANY NATIVES PRAY*

Horatio ALGER
WHO MADE A FORTUNE WRITING 119 BOOKS INSPIRING POOR BOYS TO LABOR DILIGENTLY AND SAVE THEIR PENNIES, *DIED IN POVERTY BECAUSE HE BECAME A SPENDTHRIFT*

ALLIGATORS
HAVE LONGER HIND LEGS THAN THEY HAVE IN FRONT-- *INDICATING THEIR ANCESTORS ONCE WALKED UPRIGHT*

THE CASTLE OF ALVITO
Portugal, HAS WALLS *10 FEET THICK*

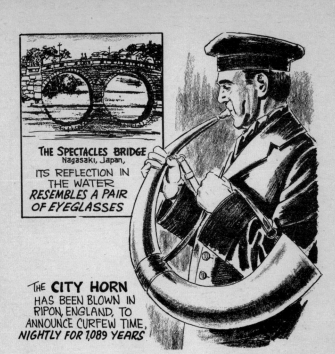

THE SPECTACLES BRIDGE
Nagasaki, Japan,
ITS REFLECTION IN
THE WATER
*RESEMBLES A PAIR
OF EYEGLASSES*

THE **CITY HORN**
HAS BEEN BLOWN IN
RIPON, ENGLAND, TO
ANNOUNCE CURFEW TIME,
NIGHTLY FOR 1,089 YEARS

THE
**MALE GAFF-TOPSAIL
CATFISH**
AFTER THE FEMALE
LAYS HER EGGS,
CARRIES THEM IN HIS
MOUTH UNTIL THEY
HATCH -- *GOING
WITHOUT FOOD
FOR 80 DAYS*

KATY JACKSON and **ESTHER COTTON**
SISTERS, 76 AND 56 YEARS OF AGE,
LIVED FOR 10 YEARS IN ROSEBURG, ORE.,
A CITY OF 14,000·· **WITHOUT KNOWING
THEY WERE SISTERS** (1961-1971)
Submitted by Bill Schneider, Kerrville, Texas

CEDAR TREE
GROWING IN THE FORK
OF A MAPLE TREE
Submitted by
Eva Segar,
Hamilton, Mo.

COUNT CHRISTIAN
of Leiningen-Heidesheim,
RULED OBERSTEIN,
GERMANY, FROM
1698 TO 1766 -- *A*
PERIOD OF 68 YEARS

THE
QUEEN of the **NIGHT**
A CACTUS THAT
BLOOMS AT MIDNIGHT,
HAS A PERFUME SO
POWERFUL, IT CAN
BE DETECTED HALF
A MILE AWAY

THE **CASTLE THAT WAS DESTROYED**
3 TIMES -- *BY ITS OWNER!*
CASTLE DANGEROUS in Scotland,
MADE FAMOUS BY SIR WALTER
SCOTT'S NOVEL OF THAT NAME,
WAS SEIZED AND GARRISONED
BY ENGLISH SOLDIERS THREE
TIMES IN THE 14th CENTURY.
ITS OWNER, SIR JAMES DOUGLAS,
ATTACKED HIS OWN CASTLE,
DEFEATED ITS DEFENDERS AND
BURNED IT TO THE GROUND

THE CAHOW
A BIRD OF THE PETREL FAMILY, *STAYS OUT TO SEA 8 MONTHS OF EACH YEAR.* IT HAS A STRANGE, WILD CRY WHICH IT UTTERS ONLY WHEN APPROACHING ITS BREEDING GROUNDS IN BERMUDA

THE GREEN WINE OF MINHO, Portugal, COMES FROM GRAPES THAT ARE SHADED BY TREES AROUND THE TRUNKS OF WHICH THE VINES GROW TO A HEIGHT OF 30 FEET

JOHN STUART MILL
ENGLISH ECONOMIST AND PHILOSOPHER, LEARNED GREEK AT THE AGE OF 3 -- STUDIED PLATO'S DIALOGUES AT 7 -- *AND TAUGHT HIS SISTER LATIN WHEN HE WAS 8*

JOHN NEWBERY
(1713-1767) AN ENGLISH PUBLISHER, WAS THE FIRST TO PRODUCE BOOKS FOR CHILDREN--PUBLISHING *"MOTHER GOOSE MELODIES"* *AND "GOODY-TWO-SHOES"*

THE **OX** TOWER at Imsum, Germany, USED AS A LANDMARK BY MARINERS, WAS ORIGINALLY *THE BELFRY OF A CHURCH*

FRANÇOIS **BARBÉ-MARBOIS**
(1745-1837)
NAPOLEON'S SECRETARY OF THE TREASURY WHO SOLD LOUISIANA TO THE U.S., WAS A PUBLIC OFFICIAL IN FRANCE FOR 66 YEARS *--SERVING AN EMPEROR AND 5 KINGS*

A **$20 BILL**
GIVEN IN CHANGE BY THE VALLEY FALLS, KANSAS, BANK TO KEN FERRELL WHO IS EMPLOYED IN GARDENA, CALIF., HAD BEEN SOMEHOW STAMPED LIKE A PIECE OF MAIL BY THE *POST OFFICE OF GARDENA, CALIF.*
Submitted by Joyce E. Widoff, Hollywood, Calif.

44

THE WORLD'S FIRST IRON BRIDGE

THE AN-CHI BRIDGE AT CHAO-HSIEN, HOPEI PROVINCE, CHINA, IS AN IRON SPAN CONSTRUCTED 1,365 YEARS AGO

DR. IGNAZ SEMMELWEIS (1818-1865) of Austria, WHO SAVED THE LIVES OF THOUSANDS OF WOMEN BY DIAGNOSING PUERPERAL FEVER AS BLOOD POISONING DUE TO AN INFECTION, *DIED OF BLOOD POISONING FROM AN INFECTED WOUND*

THE PHAESTUS DISK

A MYSTERIOUS CLAY RECORD MARKED WITH 45 HIEROGLYPHICS, WAS PRINTED WITH MOVABLE TYPE MORE *THAN 3,000 YEARS AGO*

A MAN AND A CHIMPANZEE HAVE EQUALLY HAIRY HANDS. *THE MAN'S HANDS SEEM TO HAVE LESS HAIR ONLY BECAUSE HIS HAIR IS FINER AND SHORTER*

DARTMOUTH COLLEGE
OF HANOVER, NEW HAMPSHIRE,
CONSIDERED A COLLEGE IN THE
WILDERNESS IN 1779,
CHARGED AS ITS TUITION
$13.^{32} A YEAR

A PHOTOGRAPH--
MADE BY 3 KEYS
KEYS LEFT IN A
DRAWER BETWEEN
A URANIUM-
BEARING ROCK
AND A BOX OF
PHOTOGRAPHIC
PAPER--*TOOK
THEIR OWN PHOTO*

(Buller River
District, N.Z.)

THE CEMETERY OF THE HANGED
A BURIAL PLACE BEHIND THE OLD SULTAN'S PALACE (ISTANBUL, TURKEY)
RESERVED FOR VISITORS TO THE PALACE **WHO WERE INNOCENT
OF WRONGDOING BUT WERE HANGED ON THE SULTAN'S WHIM**

THE SCULPTURED HEAD

OF A MAYA WARRIOR FOUND IN THE RUINS OF Palenque, Mexico, IN ADDITION TO FLOWERS AND FEATHERS IS ADORNED WITH A FALSE NOSE *-TO GIVE THE SUBJECT A PROFILE LIKE THE SACRED QUETZAL BIRD*

THE BUILDING THAT COST LESS THAN THE ARCHITECT'S ESTIMATE

THE EMPIRE STATE BUILDING IN NEW YORK CITY WAS COMPLETED IN 1931 FOR JUST UNDER $41,000,000— $9,000,000 LESS THAN THE ESTIMATED CONSTRUCTION COST

THE COURTHOUSE in Sydney, Australia, WAS ORIGINALLY A HOSPITAL BUILT IN 1811 BY A GROUP OF CITIZENS WHO WERE COMPENSATED BY PERMISSION FROM THE GOVERNMENT TO IMPORT **45,000 GALLONS OF WHISKEY**

RUDOLPH SCHRADER
of Berwyn, Ill., RIDING
A BICYCLE DAILY AT
THE AGE OF 100
Submitted by Jules H. Marr,
Albuquerque, N.M.

THE **WEDDING TOWER**
IN DARMSTADT, GERMANY,
WAS BUILT TO COMMEMORATE
*GRAND DUKE ERNEST LUDWIG'S
SECOND WEDDING*

THE **TOMB** of EMPEROR YUNG LE
- PEIPING, CHINA -
SINCE HIS DEATH 551 YEARS AGO,
HAS BECOME FRAMED
BY ODD-SHAPED TREES

"**GOOD**" IS WRITTEN
IN CHINESE BY
COMBINING THE CHARACTER
FOR "WOMAN" 女
WITH THAT FOR
"CHILD" 子
-- 女子

48

THE CATHEDRAL OF SALAMANCA
Spain
WAS UNDER CONSTRUCTION
FOR 220 YEARS

WOMEN of Yap Island, WEAR A **30-LB.** SKIRT OF SWEET, SCENTED GRASS-- WHICH THEY OFTEN SHARE WITH AN ASSORTMENT OF **CENTI-PEDES, SPIDERS AND BEETLES**

THE CASTLE OF CAPE TOWN So. Africa, BUILT IN 1666, AND NOW SERVING AS HEAD-QUARTERS OF THE SO. AFRICAN DEFENSE FORCE IS THE *COUNTRY'S OLDEST STRUCTURE*

M.E. KELLOGG DIED A NATURAL DEATH

Epitaph IN BOOT HILL CEMETERY, TOMBSTONE, ARIZ.

WILLIAM BONNY THE NOTORIOUS KILLER KNOWN AS BILLY THE KID, *ACTUALLY WAS A STOOL PIGEON* WHO VOLUNTARILY TESTIFIED AGAINST FELLOW BADMEN IN RETURN FOR A PROMISE OF PERSONAL IMMUNITY ON OTHER MURDER CHARGES

I'LL LOOK UPON JOHNNY IN MY POOL IN JULY IN HILLY HONOLULU.

A SENTENCE THAT CAN BE TYPED BY TOUCH-TYPING *ENTIRELY WITH THE RIGHT HAND*

THE **CATHEDRAL OF TARRAGONA** Spain, WAS BUILT ON THE FOUNDATIONS OF A MOHAMMEDAN MOSQUE WHICH HAD BEEN ERECTED ON THE *FOUNDATION OF A HEATHEN TEMPLE TO JUPITER*

ENOUGH'S ENOUGH!

A **MAILBOX** AT MADISON AND HALSTED STS., CHICAGO, ILL. AVERAGES *8,700 PIECES* OF MAIL A DAY-- *--1,400 POUNDS OF MAIL A WEEK*

A **SNAIL** DOES NOT CRAWL--*IT WALKS ON ONE LEG*

TESTIMONIAL TO ECOLOGY

GOOD WATER,
A LOT OF EXERCISE
AND GOOD AIR
WERE THE REASON
THAT I ENTERED THIS
GRAVE SO LATE

Epitaph of DR. FRIEDRICH B. KRUPP
WHO DIED AT THE AGE OF 91.
Iserlohn, Germany

THE **LIGHTHOUSE** of Lissewege, Belgium,

BUILT IN 1250...
5 CENTURIES
LATER BECAME
*THE BELFRY OF
THE LOCAL
CHURCH*

*EASY COME,
EASY GO !*
Francis X. Bushman
IDOL OF THE SILENT
SCREEN BETWEEN
1912 AND 1918,
MADE MORE THAN
$6,000,000
IN TAX-FREE DOLLARS--
AND ENDED UP BROKE!

A **FEMALE POLAR BEAR**
WHEN THREATENED, OFTEN GIVES HER
YOUNG A **PIGGYBACK RIDE TO SAFETY**

THEODORE POMEROY
(1825-1905) OF NEW YORK, IN THE 40th SESSION OF CONGRESS IN 1869, SERVED AS SPEAKER OF THE HOUSE *FOR A SINGLE DAY*

THE **JUNGFRAUJOCH HOTEL**
ON A RIDGE OF MOUNT JUNGFRAU IN SWITZERLAND, *IS BUILT INTO A CAVE IN THE SOLID ROCK*

SUSAN REYNOLDS
OF PRESTWICH, ENGLAND, WHO AT 19 CAN READ **22** LANGUAGES, COULD READ ENGLISH AT **2**, WROTE A HISTORICAL NOVEL AT **14** AND *ENTERED OXFORD AT 16*

THE RICHEST MAN IN HISTORY!
King Ptolemy Philadelphus
(309-246 B.C.) of Egypt,
HAD AT HIS DISPOSAL A TREASURY
OF 740,000 TALENTS -- THE EQUIVALENT
IN PURCHASING POWER TODAY TO
$90,280,000,000

THE **PAGODA** OF **YU-CHHUAN**
IN HOPEI PROVINCE, CHINA,
BUILT IN 1061 *WAS MADE OF CAST IRON*

I'LL SUE!

AN **APPEAL FOR ELEGANCE**
RUN IN THE PUBLICATION
"BROOKLYN LIFE," IN 1890,
REQUESTED "**HOMELY
PEOPLE**" TO STAY OUT
OF THE EASTER PARADE

THE **SALT MARSH HARVEST MOUSE**
OF CALIF., IS ONLY **3 INCHES**
LONG, BUT IT HAS A **3½-INCH TAIL**

THE **GRAVE** OF A WOMAN
OF THE IBIBIO TRIBE OF
SO. NIGERIA, IS MARKED
WITH HER KITCHEN POTS, HER
MARKET BASKET AND HER PILLOW

A CHINESE CLOCK CARVED IN HARD-WOOD IN THE 14th CENTURY, CONTAINS A MAZE OF GROOVES THAT WERE FILLED WITH A VARIETY OF AROMATIC INCENSES-- *EACH OF WHICH WOULD BURN FOR 12 HOURS*

FASHIONABLE WOMEN IN THE 15th CENTURY, PLUCKED THEIR EYEBROWS AND *SHAVED THEIR UPPER FOREHEADS*

HORSE'S HEAD NEAR MYWATN, ICELAND, *NATURAL ROCK FORMATION*

THE BELFRY OF THE CATHEDRAL OF THE HOLY CROSS, IN SWABIAN GMÜND, GERMANY, *IS 500 YEARS OLDER THAN THE CHURCH--WHICH WAS BUILT BESIDE IT* (1351)

THE CLOCK
ON THE CITY HALL OF ORANGE, FRANCE, AFTER STRIKING 5 O'CLOCK EACH AFTERNOON, SOUNDS AN ALARM TO NOTIFY THE CITIZENRY *IT IS TIME TO WASH THE STREET IN FRONT OF THEIR HOMES*

WARRIORS
OF THE ASMAT TRIBE OF NEW GUINEA, USE AS A PILLOW *THE SKULLS OF THEIR FATHERS*

THE NEW YORK STOCK EXCHANGE
IN NEW YORK CITY, IN 1827, OCCUPIED ONE ROOM IN THE MERCHANTS' EXCHANGE BUILDING -- *FOR AN ANNUAL RENTAL OF $500*

THE FIRST ELECTROMAGNETIC TELEGRAPH
WHICH SENT SIGNALS THROUGH A MILE OF WIRE, WAS BUILT BY JOSEPH HENRY IN 1831 -- *6 YEARS BEFORE MORSE'S TELEGRAPH*

THE MASON BEE

DEPOSITS EACH EGG IN AN EMPTY SNAIL SHELL -- THEN FILLS THE SHELL WITH POLLEN AND NECTAR AND SEALS IT WITH CHEWED LEAVES TO GUARD AGAINST PREDATORS

MAKING USE OF BORROWED TIME

CECIL RHODES, THE ENGLISHMAN WHO BECAME THE MOST POWERFUL MAN IN SO. AFRICA, AMASSED A FORTUNE AND HAD NORTHERN AND SOUTHERN RHODESIA NAMED AFTER HIM, AS A STUDENT WAS GIVEN *ONLY 6 MONTHS TO LIVE*

THE MINARET OF DJAM

in Afghanistan, **206** FEET HIGH, IS ALL THAT REMAINS OF FIROZKOH, ONCE THE EMPIRE'S CAPITAL WHICH WAS *DESTROYED BY AN EARTHQUAKE*

THE SWIFT

THE FASTEST OF ALL SMALL BIRDS, *CAN FLY 170 M.P.H.*

A CASHMERE GOAT

IN A SINGLE CLIPPING PROVIDES *ONLY 3 OUNCES OF CASHMERE FLEECE*

DISK-SHAPED TOMBSTONES ARE USED BY BASQUES OF FRANCE AND SPAIN AS A LINK TO ANCESTORS WHO WERE *SUN WORSHIPERS*

NICOLAS PIETRI (1863-1964) of Sartena, Corsica, GIVEN THE NAME OF AN OLDER BROTHER WHO DIED AT THE AGE OF ONE -- *LIVED TO THE AGE OF 101*

THE NATIONAL MUSEUM -Rome, Italy- ONE OF THE WORLD'S RICHEST, WAS ORIGINALLY BUILT IN 305 AS THE *BATHS OF EMPEROR DIOCLETIAN*

THE CLUB USED IN CHOLE, AN ANCIENT FRENCH AND BELGIAN GAME SIMILAR TO GOLF, HAD A LOFTED FRONT FOR HITTING THE BALL FROM BAD LIES- *BUT ITS SIDE WAS USED FOR LONG SHOTS*

THE BATH WHITE BUTTERFLY WAS NAMED AFTER AN EMBROIDERED SAMPLER FOUND IN BATH, ENGLAND, *TO WHICH IT BORE A REMARKABLE RESEMBLANCE*

NATIVES of Liberia, Africa, SUSPECTED OF A CRIME, ONCE HAD A HOT IRON APPLIED TO THEIR TONGUE *—AND WERE ADJUDGED GUILTY IF IT BLISTERED*

THE CATHEDRAL OF MEISSEN
Germany
STARTED IN 1220,
WAS COMPLETED IN 1912
--692 YEARS LATER

CHILDREN OF THE AFRICAN GOLD COAST OFTEN BALANCE ON THEIR HEADS THEIR TEXTBOOKS AND ALSO *A BOTTLE OF INK*

THE GUZLA
A ONE-STRINGED MUSICAL INSTRUMENT OF YUGOSLAVIA, IS MADE FROM *A SINGLE BLOCK OF WOOD*

THE **ACROBATIC FOLK DANCERS OF PUNJAB** -India-
THE BHANGRA, A FOLK DANCE PERFORMED IN PUNJAB, REQUIRES EACH PARTICIPANT TO DANCE ON A PIECE OF POTTERY *BALANCED ON ANOTHER MAN'S HEAD*

MULBERRY TREE WITH A *TRIPLE-KNOTTED TRUNK*
Submitted by Aina L. Anderson
Ravena, N.Y.

RABBIT EARS
COLUMBIA RIVER GORGE, OREGON,
NATURAL ROCK FORMATION

BEES IN SPARSELY FLOWERED AREAS, FLY **300,000** MILES TO COLLECT ONE POUND OF HONEY

A **ROMAN COLUMN** IN AVENCHES, SWITZERLAND —THE ONLY ONE IN THE COUNTRY *STILL STANDING ON ITS ORIGINAL SITE*

HITLER WAS A DRAFT EVADER!

ADOLPH HITLER

IN MAY 1913, TO AVOID CONSCRIPTION IN THE AUSTRIAN ARMY, SLIPPED ACROSS THE GERMAN BORDER INTO MUNICH-- BUT WAS ARRESTED AND TURNED OVER TO THE AUSTRIAN POLICE

HE WAS NOT PROSECUTED AND FAILED THE DRAFT PHYSICAL EXAM, BUT AT THE OUTBREAK OF WORLD WAR I A YEAR LATER, VOLUNTEERED IN THE GERMAN ARMY

OH, NO!

PEARL-BEARING MUSSELS WERE FOUND IN THE EARLY 1850'S IN NOTCH BROOK, 3 MILES FROM PATERSON, N.J. -- *INCLUDING A $25,000 PEARL THAT WAS RUINED BECAUSE THE MUSSEL WAS COOKED BEFORE THE PEARL'S DISCOVERY*

INDIAN HEAD ROCK Highway 73, BETWEEN TOWNSEND AND GATLINBURG, TENNESSEE

Submitted by BILL GILLAND, GATLINBURG

THE **EXPLOSION** at Braamfontein, S. Africa, OF HALF A MILLION STICKS OF DYNAMITE, WAS HEARD IN KLERKSDORP, *100 MILES AWAY* (1896)

BLACK BART

ONE OF THE OLD WEST'S MOST NOTORIOUS ROAD AGENTS, ALWAYS DRESSED LIKE A BUSINESS-MAN -- *AND NEVER FIRED HIS GUN*

THE **STUD THORN** OF RHODESIA, AFRICA, WHEN ITS FLOWER IS BOILED, *YIELDS SOAP*

THE **TOMB** IN AURANGABAD, INDIA, OF PRINCESS RABIA DAURANI, DAUGHTER OF INDIAN EMPEROR AURANGZEB, *IS A SMALL REPLICA OF THE TAJ MAHAL*

MORICZ SANDOR A HUNGARIAN EQUESTRIAN, JUMPED HIS HORSE, COQUETTE, *OVER A WALL 8 FEET, 3 INCHES HIGH IN 1836*

THE **CHAPEL OF OTTMARSHEIM** IN Alsace, France, BUILT IN 1049, WAS CONSTRUCTED AS A FAITHFUL REPLICA OF CHARLEMAGNE'S CHAPEL, ERECTED IN AACHEN, GERMANY, *250 YEARS EARLIER*

THE **REV. DAVID PACHER** (1816-1902) OF OBERVELLACH, AUSTRIA, SERVED AS A PASTOR FOR *62 YEARS*

THE **HEART** IN ANCIENT EGYPTIAN HIEROGLYPHICS IS PORTRAYED BY THE OUTLINE OF THE *TYPE OF VASE IN WHICH PHARAOHS' HEARTS WERE BURIED*

TROBRIAND ISLANDERS of New Guinea, PRY FISH OUT OF HOLES IN THE CORAL IN DEEP WATER, *WITH SMALL STICKS*

THE **CASTLE** near Jonsdorf, Germany, *NATURAL ROCK FORMATION*

A **LUBA** WOMAN of Africa, WEAVES REEDS INTO HER HAIRDO TO ANNOUNCE THAT HER BABY HAS *CUT ITS FIRST TEETH*

A COUNTRY STORE ON THE SORLAND COAST OF NORWAY, LOCATED ON AN OTHERWISE UNINHABITED ROCKY ISLAND, CAN *BE REACHED ONLY BY BOAT*

WILLIAM EDWARD ROWLANDS (1839-1927) WAS A MINISTER FOR 66 YEARS-- SERVING *37 YEARS IN CEYLON, AND 29 IN ENGLAND*

LEO SHOWALTER of Vancouver, Wash.,

PLAYING GOLF AT THE ROYAL OAKS C.C. *MADE A HOLE-IN-ONE TWICE ON THE SAME HOLE IN A PERIOD OF ONLY 4 DAYS*

Submitted by Emery F. Tobin, Vancouver

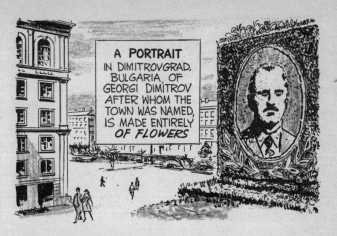

A PORTRAIT IN DIMITROVGRAD, BULGARIA, OF GEORGI DIMITROV AFTER WHOM THE TOWN WAS NAMED, IS MADE ENTIRELY *OF FLOWERS*

THE PRINTING PRESS OF JOHANN GUTENBERG --*THE WORLD'S FIRST*-- *WAS LOST FOR 388 YEARS AFTER HIS DEATH IN 1468*

KING **RAMESES II** WHO RULED EGYPT FOR 67 YEARS AND DIED AT THE AGE OF 90, OUTLIVED *12 OF HIS SONS*

ROGER BROOKE TANEY
WHO SERVED FOR 28 YEARS AS
CHIEF JUSTICE OF THE U.S. (1836-64)
HAD PREVIOUSLY BEEN
REJECTED BY THE SENATE
AS AN ASSOCIATE JUSTICE

THE **CHURCH** of **INARI**, Finland,
A WILDERNESS STRUCTURE OF
WOOD, HOLDS SERVICES
ONLY ONCE A YEAR

AN **AMPHIBIOUS STEAMER**
30 FEET LONG AND
WEIGHING **15** TONS,
BUILT IN 1804 BY OLIVER
EVANS FOR THE BOARD OF
HEALTH IN PHILADELPHIA, PA.,
*WAS AMERICA'S FIRST WHEELED
VEHICLE CAPABLE OF MOVING
UNDER ITS OWN POWER*

THE **GRAVE** OF A
LHOTA NAGA WARRIOR of India, IS
ADORNED BY A ROW OF WOODEN
BALLS--*EACH REPRESENTING THE HEAD
OF AN ENEMY CUT OFF IN BATTLE*

A
**GOLD
WATCH**
MADE
IN
GENEVA,
SWITZER-
LAND, IN 1810,
IN THE
SHAPE OF
A HARP

66

THE **GENDARME**
MACHAPUCHARE MT., NEPAL,
A PEAK THAT LOOKS LIKE
**THE STONY FACE OF
A POLICEMAN**

HANS CHRISTIAN ANDERSEN

(1805-1875) FAMED DANISH
CREATOR OF FAIRY TALES,
WRITING HIS FIRST BOOK,
"Ghost of Palanatoke's Tomb,"
USED THE PSEUDONYM WILLIAM
CHRISTIAN WALTER, BORROWING
FOR HIS FIRST AND LAST NAMES THOSE
OF THE WRITERS HE MOST ADMIRED
-- *WILLIAM SHAKESPEARE
AND WALTER SCOTT*

A **COUNTERSTAMP**
ADDED TO A
SOUTH AMERICAN
DOLLAR, WAS THE
MEANS BY WHICH THE
DOWAGER COUNTESS
OF ORMONDE, IRELAND,
*ISSUED HER OWN
MONEY IN 1804*

THE "**COAT
OF ARMS**"
of Storkow,
Germany,
IS A LIVING
PAIR OF STORKS
--*AND 2 STORKS
HAVE SHARED A
SPECIAL PLATFORM
ABOVE THE TOWN
HALL FOR 766 YEARS*

EMIL JANNINGS
GERMANY'S MOST FAMOUS
MOVIE STAR, WAS BORN
IN BROOKLYN, N.Y.

THE **OCTAGON TOWER**
OF THE RUINED
CASTLE OF
Steinsberg, Germany,
*HAS WALLS
13 FEET THICK*

FREDENS CHURCH
IN ODENSE, DENMARK,
WAS BUILT IN THE SHAPE
OF A CHURCH ORGAN

THE **NOMOLI**
A HUMAN
FIGURE
CARVED FROM
SOAPSTONE,
WAS BURIED
IN RICE
FIELDS IN
SIERRA LEONE,
AFRICA,
*TO ASSURE
A GOOD CROP*

The PARISH CHURCH
OF LOËX, SWITZERLAND,
IS USED ONLY
FOR FUNERALS

The MAGIC FAIRY-TALE TABLE OF CASTLE LINDERHOF
THE TABLE BUILT BY THE
BAVARIAN KING WHO CON-
STRUCTED THE CASTLE,
WAS INSPIRED BY A
FAIRY TALE ABOUT A
MAGIC TABLE --AND
*LIKE THE MYTHICAL
TABLE, CAN BE DROPPED
INTO A BASEMENT KITCHEN
AND EMERGE COVERED
WITH FOOD*

THE IMPORTANCE OF TIMING
SIR WALTER RALEIGH
WAS EXECUTED BY KING JAMES I
FOR ANNOYING SPAIN--
YET FOR DOING THE SAME THING,
*SIR FRANCIS DRAKE WAS
KNIGHTED BY QUEEN ELIZABETH*

The FIRST MAGNETIC COMPASS
A COMPASS USED BY CHINESE
SORCERERS IN 480 B.C., CONSISTED
OF A METAL PLATE ATOP A
SQUARE BASE -- *WITH A
MAGNETIZED SPOON THAT AL-
WAYS POINTED TO THE SOUTH*

THE **DOOR** of the CHURCH OF ST. PÈRE IN SANCERRE, FRANCE, IS STILL INTACT ALTHOUGH THE REST OF THE EDIFICE WAS *DESTROYED 414 YEARS AGO*

HOW TO BRING ON A BUSINESS RECESSION

Wallace Reid
THE SILENT FILM STAR, DONNED A SHIRT WITH A SOFT COLLAR IN 1922-- *AND COMPANIES THAT HAD BEEN MAKING STIFF ATTACHABLE COLLARS WERE PUT OUT OF BUSINESS*

THE **LION FISH** OF THE INDIAN OCEAN, RESEMBLES A LION AND *HAS A LETHAL STING*

2 ARCHES SPANNING THE ENTIRE ROAD AT SAMMA el BARADAN, SYRIA, ARE ALL THAT REMAIN OF THE BYZANTINE CHURCH **BUILT THERE IN THE 5th CENTURY**

THE **BELFRY** of the Church of St-Jeoire, Switzerland, STILL STANDS ALTHOUGH THE CHURCH WAS DEMOLISHED *CENTURIES AGO*

A **GIRL** IN THE KUTTIA KOND TRIBE OF ORISSA, INDIA, ADVERTISES THAT SHE IS SINGLE *BY WEARING 3 RINGS IN HER NOSE*

THE **DASSIE** of Africa, IS ONLY THE SIZE OF A GUINEA PIG --YET IT IS THE NEAREST RELATIVE OF THE ELEPHANT

THE CASTLE OF ANJONY NEAR AURILLAC, FRANCE, BUILT IN 1459, HAS BEEN OWNED BY THE SAME FAMILY *FOR 516 YEARS*

THE **FIRST ELECTRIC PLANT** IN NEW YORK CITY, WAS OPENED BY EDISON IN 1882 *WITH ONLY 59 CUSTOMERS*

ADMIRAL GEORGE RODNEY WHO WON THE BATTLE OF THE SAINTS AGAINST THE FRENCH IN 1782, *WAS THE ONLY BRITISH OFFICER TO WIN A MAJOR NAVAL BATTLE DURING THE ENTIRE AMERICAN WAR OF INDEPENDENCE*

A **PEDESTRIAN-CATCHER** TO REPLACE THE NORMAL BUMPER, *WAS INVENTED FOR CARS IN THE 1900's*

THE **OFFICIAL EXECUTION SWORD** LONG USED IN LÖWENBURG, GERMANY, BEARS THE INSCRIPTION:" WHEN I RAISE THIS SWORD I WISH THE POOR SINNER ETERNAL LIFE."

PIETRO LANDO (1461-1545) DOGE OF VENICE FROM 1539 TO 1545, ORDERED THE EXECUTION OF HIS OWN SON BECAUSE *THE YOUTH KISSED A GIRL IN PUBLIC*

THE **CASTLE OF MONTEZUMA** IN VERDE VALLEY, ARIZONA, A FORTRESS BUILT INTO A LIMESTONE CLIFF **5** STORIES HIGH WITH **20** ROOMS, IS STILL **90** PERCENT INTACT *AFTER 700 YEARS*

BRIG. GENERAL DAVID ROGERSON WILLIAMS (1776-1830) IN 1812 WAS ELECTED GOVERNOR OF SO. CAROLINA AGAINST HIS WISHES --CALLING IT THE **GREATEST MISFORTUNE OF HIS LIFE**

THE BELLTOWER OF THE CHURCH OF EKATONTAPYLIANI, PAROS, GREECE, IS MORE *THAN 1,000 YEARS OLD*

PRESIDENT JAMES A. GARFIELD COULD HAVE SURVIVED HIS ASSASSIN'S BULLET IN 1881 BECAUSE IT LODGED IN HIS BACK MUSCLES A FEW INCHES FROM ITS ENTRY POINT, *AND HIS BODY HAD ENVELOPED IT IN A PROTECTIVE CYST.* HE DIED BECAUSE DOCTORS PROBED OFF AND ON FOR **71** DAYS -- UNSTERILE INSTRUMENTS SPREADING INFECTION

THE SULEIMAN GOAT HAS VERY LONG WHISKERS AND HORNS SHAPED LIKE **CORKSCREWS**

THE **ANCIENT PAGAN TEMPLE of ISIS** in Philae, Egypt, SERVED FOR MANY YEARS AS A ***CHRISTIAN CHURCH***

ONE DOLLAR BILL ISSUED DURING THE AMERICAN CIVIL WAR BY CHEROKEE INDIANS -- *PAYABLE IN CONFEDERATE CURRENCY*

CHARLES GOODNIGHT (1836-1929) ONE OF THE LAST OF THE CATTLE DRIVERS OF THE OLD WEST, *LIVED TO THE AGE OF 93 ON A DIET OF MEAT AND COFFEE*

THE **GRAVE** OF A FISHERMAN IN VISTA, THE CONGO, IS IDENTIFIED BY A BUST OF THE DECEASED, HIS CREEL AND A *REPLICA OF HIS FISHING BOAT*

DANCING CARROTS

Submitted by Mrs. Marie Bernhardt, Hudson, Colo.

A **BIRDHOUSE** EXHIBITED FOR SALE OUTSIDE A STORE IN CHURCH CREEK MD., *WAS MOVED INTO BY A FAMILY OF PURPLE MARTINS.*

WHEN MEN WORE PETTICOATS

DANDIES IN THE 17TH CENTURY WORE VELVET BREECHES ADORNED WITH RIBBONS, AND SO FULL THAT *THEY WERE VIRTUALLY PETTICOATS*

THE **OLDEST CHESTNUT TREE IN GERMANY** THE PARK OF HERTEN CASTLE -- *PLANTED IN 1699*

TOM MORRIS, SR. COMPETED IN EVERY BRITISH OPEN GOLF CHAMPIONSHIP *FROM THE TOURNAMENT'S INCEPTION IN 1860 UNTIL 1896.* HE WON THE TITLE 4 TIMES

THE **CHAPEL OF DRUGGELT**
Germany,
CONSTRUCTED IN 1226,
IS A REPLICA OF THE
CHURCH OF THE HOLY
SEPULCHRE IN JERUSALEM

WONGGU - A NATIVE
OF ARNHEM LAND, AUSTRALIA,
AFTER A BLOOD FEUD, BECAME
THE LAST SURVIVOR OF
HIS TRIBE-- BUT HE
THEN MARRIED AND
*BECAME FATHER OF
50 CHILDREN*

VINCENT VAN GOGH
THE FAMED
DUTCH
MASTER,
SOLD ONLY
2 PAINTINGS
DURING HIS
ENTIRE
LIFETIME,
*AND NETTED
A TOTAL
OF $84*

SELF-PORTRAIT

A **WIFE** OF THE BABIRA TRIBE, AFRICA, IS CON-SIDERED DIVORCED WHEN HER HUSBAND PLACES A PITCHER OF OIL AND A STAFF OUTSIDE THEIR HUT

THE **AVERAGE** FAMILY IN THE UNITED STATES CONSUMES 2½ TONS OF FOOD EACH YEAR

KING HUSSEIN (1675-1729) of Persia, BECAUSE HE BECAME FOND OF HIS PET DUCKS, FORBADE THE KILLING OF ANY DUCK THROUGHOUT HIS KINGDOM *UNDER PAIN OF DEATH*

MRS. **JULEEN STOWE** of Thomasville, N.C., WHO WAS THE FIRST BABY BORN IN LORIS, S.C. ON NEW YEAR'S DAY 1954, *BECAME THE MOTHER OF THE FIRST CHILD BORN IN HIGH POINT, N.C., ON NEW YEAR'S DAY 1975*

THE WORLD'S TALLEST TOTEM POLE

"THE TOTEM POLE OF THE MOUNTAIN CHIEF," NOW IN THE ROYAL ONTARIO MUSEUM, TORONTO, ONTARIO, IS **80½ FEET HIGH**

THE **FLORAL CLOCK** in Ballarat, Australia, HAS ITS NUMERALS AND ENTIRE FACE *IN BRILLIANT BLOOMS*

STATUE OF SAINT CLEMENT

IN THE CHURCH OF SANTA MARIA, IN VISSANI, ITALY, CONTAINS THE SAINT'S BODY, PRESERVED BY A COATING OF WAX

79

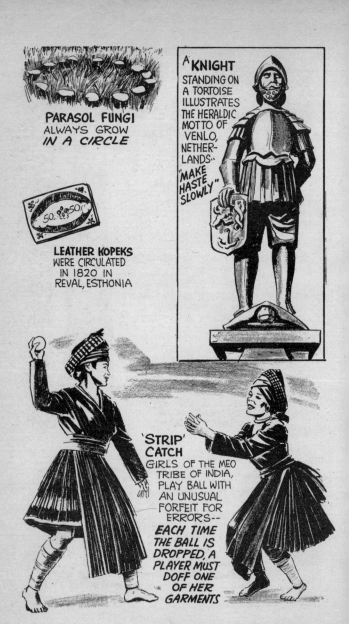

PARASOL FUNGI
ALWAYS GROW
IN A CIRCLE

LEATHER KOPEKS
WERE CIRCULATED
IN 1820 IN
REVAL, ESTHONIA

A **KNIGHT**
STANDING ON
A TORTOISE
ILLUSTRATES
THE HERALDIC
MOTTO OF
VENLO,
NETHER-
LANDS"
*"MAKE
HASTE
SLOWLY"*

**'STRIP'
CATCH**
GIRLS OF THE MEO
TRIBE OF INDIA,
PLAY BALL WITH
AN UNUSUAL
FORFEIT FOR
ERRORS--
*EACH TIME
THE BALL IS
DROPPED, A
PLAYER MUST
DOFF ONE
OF HER
GARMENTS*

NATURAL PAVING BLOCKS
KIRKJUBAEJÁRKLAUSTRI, Iceland, A STRETCH OF GROUND THAT LOOKS LIKE THE STONE FLOOR OF A CHURCH, *ACTUALLY IS A FORMATION OF LAVA COLUMNS*

LUKE ROBERTS of Douglas, Nebraska, STARTED SAVING STRING AT THE AGE OF **81** — AND IN **5 YEARS** FORMED A BALL OF STRING WEIGHING **300 POUNDS**

THE **HEADGEAR** OF ARAB WOMEN IN SOUTHERN ISRAEL, OFTEN IS TRIMMED WITH SILVER COINS *AS EVIDENCE OF THEIR SOLVENCY*

HENRY CLAY THE "GREAT COMPROMISER," WAS ELECTED SPEAKER OF THE HOUSE OF REPRESENTATIVES ON *THE FIRST DAY HE ENTERED THAT CHAMBER*

THE HORNBOOK

USED IN ALL ENGLISH SCHOOLS IN THE 16th AND 17th CENTURIES, WAS A BOARD ON WHICH THE ALPHABET OR OTHER LESSON WAS PASTED UNDER A PIECE OF CLEAR HORN TO PROTECT *THE THEN PRECIOUS PAPER*

THE FIRST MALPRACTICE JUDGMENTS

King Hammurabi, WHO RULED BABYLONIA FOR 43 YEARS, ESTABLISHED A CODE FOR DOCTORS WHICH SPECIFIED THAT IF A NOBLEMAN LOST HIS SIGHT, HIS *PHYSICIAN LOST A HAND*

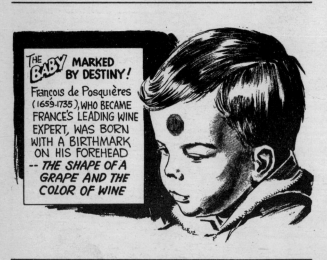

THE BABY MARKED BY DESTINY!

François de Posquières (1659-1735), WHO BECAME FRANCE'S LEADING WINE EXPERT, WAS BORN WITH A BIRTHMARK ON HIS FOREHEAD -- *THE SHAPE OF A GRAPE AND THE COLOR OF WINE*

THE **MONK** WHO PREDICTED HIS OWN DEATH!
Simon de Roxas (1552-1624) A SPANISH MONK, ON SEPT. 28, 1614, AT 7:45 A.M., PREDICTED THAT HIS DEATH WOULD OCCUR 10 YEARS LATER... *HE DIED ON SEPT. 28, 1624 AT 7:45 A.M.*

MINOU DROUET of Paris, France, HAD HER FIRST BOOK OF POEMS PUBLISHED *WHEN SHE WAS 9 YEARS OF AGE*

PAULINE E. TAYLOR and **PAULINE TAYLOR** of Detroit, Michigan, WERE BORN WITHIN 2 HOURS OF EACH OTHER AS ALMOST IDENTICAL LOOK-ALIKES AND DEVELOPED THE SAME TASTES IN DRESS, FOOD, CLOTHES AND HOBBIES, --*YET WERE IN NO WAY RELATED*

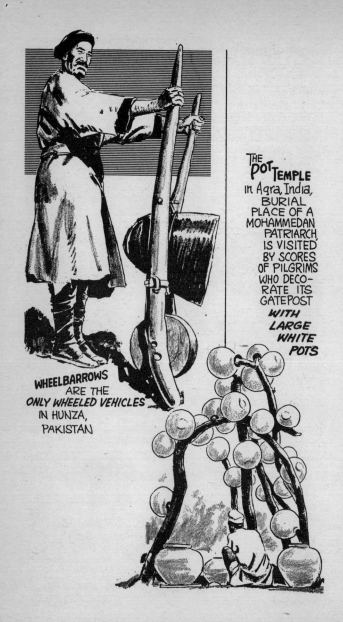

THE **POT** TEMPLE
in Agra, India,
BURIAL
PLACE OF A
MOHAMMEDAN
PATRIARCH,
IS VISITED
BY SCORES
OF PILGRIMS
WHO DECO-
RATE ITS
GATEPOST
WITH
LARGE
WHITE
POTS

WHEELBARROWS
ARE THE
ONLY WHEELED VEHICLES
IN HUNZA,
PAKISTAN

JOHN WILKES BOOTH

WHO SHOT PRESIDENT LINCOLN, LIKE ALL OTHER ACTORS OF THE CIVIL WAR PERIOD, *HAD DIPLOMATIC IMMUNITY*

KING HENRY VIII CREATED A STYLE OF WEARING SLASHED SHOES THAT WAS THE MALE FASHION FOR 150 YEARS-- *BECAUSE HE SUFFERED FROM ACHING CORNS*

MOVE OVER, RIP VAN WINKLE! AN ADULT, 70 YEARS OF AGE, HAS SPENT 25 YEARS OF HIS LIFE SLEEPING

A MODEL of the DECEASED'S HOME IS CREMATED WITH THE DEPARTED AT A CHINESE FUNERAL SO THE SOUL WILL HAVE A FAMILIAR ABODE

FASHIONABLE GENTLEMEN IN 17th CENTURY FRANCE, DONNED 2 PAIRS OF SHOES --WEARING HEELED SHOES INSIDE A PAIR OF SLIPPERS

THE SAME BUILDING IN VÖRSTETTEN, GERMANY, SERVES AS THE TOWN'S *SCHOOL, CITY HALL AND CHURCH*

A *STONE* CONTAINING A NATURAL 5-POINTED STAR
Submitted by Karen Covella, Rochester, N.Y.

MAURITZ PRETORIUS OF THE CAPE COLONY OF SOUTH AFRICA, *BECAME A FATHER AND A GREAT-GREAT GRAND-FATHER ON THE SAME DAY*

EVA HIRDLER RECEIVED HER EARNED DEGREE IN MINING ENGINEERING FROM THE MISSOURI SCHOOL OF MINES AND METALLURGY *AT THE AGE OF 88--61 YEARS AFTER LEAVING THE SCHOOL*

Submitted by JULES HENRY MARR Albuquerque, N.M.

87

THE ELEPHANT'S HEAD
Ausable Chasm, N.Y.
NATURAL ROCK FORMATION

AN APACHE SQUAW IN GERONIMO'S TRIBE, WAS PUNISHED FOR BEING UNFAITHFUL BY CUTTING OFF THE TIP OF HER NOSE

THE CHURCH OF TORRICELLA, Italy, BUILT IN THE 11th CENTURY, IS NOW OCCUPIED AS A FARMHOUSE

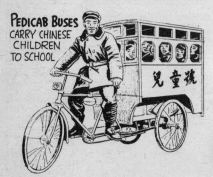

PEDICAB BUSES CARRY CHINESE CHILDREN TO SCHOOL

兒童號

FREDERICK THE GREAT, A FROG OWNED BY MARTIN WALTER of Cleveland, Ohio, WAS TRAINED TO SMOKE A CIGARET

88

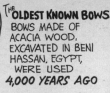

THE OLDEST KNOWN BOWS BOWS MADE OF ACACIA WOOD, EXCAVATED IN BENI HASSAN, EGYPT, WERE USED *4,000 YEARS AGO*

THE LIGHTHOUSE ON LAKE CORRIB, BALLYCURRAN, IRELAND, IS THE ONLY LIGHTHOUSE ON AN INLAND WATERWAY IN *THE ENTIRE BRITISH ISLES*

ARMAND de RANCE (1626-1700) WAS THE ABBOT OF 4 RELIGIOUS ORDERS AT *THE AGE OF 11*

THE AOUDAD AFRICA'S WILD SHEEP, IS EQUALLY AT HOME ON THE CRAGS OF THE ATLAS MTS., AT 13,000 FT., AND ON THE SUN-BAKED SAHARA DESERT

WATERFALL IN Assam, India, CREATED BY AN EARTHQUAKE IN 1897 --*AND STILL RUNNING 78 YEARS LATER*

THE **TOMB** NEAR THE PORTA MAGGIORE IN ROME, ITALY, OF M. VERGILIUS EURYSACES, A MILLER AND BAKER, WHO DIED 1,900 YEARS AGO, IS A REPLICA OF HIS OVEN

PRESIDENT CHESTER ALAN ARTHUR REFUSED TO MOVE INTO THE WHITE HOUSE IN 1881 UNTIL 24 WAGONLOADS OF FURNITURE AND DECORATIONS --INCLUDING SOME PRICELESS ANTIQUES-- HAD BEEN REMOVED

A **MOTHER-IN-LAW** AMONG THE NAVAHO INDIANS IS FORBIDDEN TO SPEAK TO HER DAUGHTER'S HUSBAND

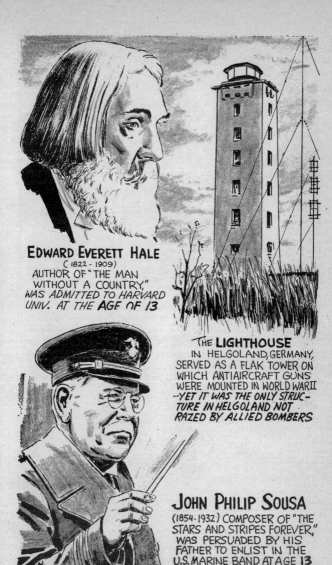

EDWARD EVERETT HALE
(1822 - 1909)
AUTHOR OF " THE MAN
WITHOUT A COUNTRY,"
WAS ADMITTED TO HARVARD
UNIV. AT THE *AGE OF 13*

THE **LIGHTHOUSE**
IN HELGOLAND, GERMANY,
SERVED AS A FLAK TOWER ON
WHICH ANTIAIRCRAFT GUNS
WERE MOUNTED IN WORLD WAR II
--*YET IT WAS THE ONLY STRUC-
TURE IN HELGOLAND NOT
RAZED BY ALLIED BOMBERS*

JOHN PHILIP SOUSA
(1854-1932) COMPOSER OF "THE
STARS AND STRIPES FOREVER,"
WAS PERSUADED BY HIS
FATHER TO ENLIST IN THE
U.S. MARINE BAND AT AGE *13*
--*HIS FATHER FEARED HIS
SON PLANNED TO BECOME
A CIRCUS MUSICIAN*

THE **ELEPHANT** NORTHERN AUSTRALIA, *UNIQUELY SHAPED ANT HILL*

DOLLS IN AFGHANISTAN, ARE MADE OF DRIED APRICOTS STRUNG TOGETHER ON CORDS WITH PIECES OF COLORED CLOTH AS EYES

THE **NOTRE DAME CHURCH** IN SEMUR-EN-AUSSOIS, FRANCE, WAS CONSTRUCTED BY THE DUKE OF BOURGOGNE IN 1060, *AS EXPIATION FOR HAVING SLAIN HIS FATHER-IN-LAW IN A QUARREL*

HAIRPINS IN THE CENTRAL CONGO, *ONCE SERVED AS CURRENCY*

A PUBLIC RELIEF PROJECT-- INDIAN STYLE THE MOSQUE OF ASAF-ud-DAULA in Lucknow, India, WAS BUILT BY SULTAN ASAF-ud-DAULA IN 1775, *TO GIVE HIS SUBJECTS WORK DURING A SEVERE FAMINE*

THE WOMAN WHO WAS ABE LINCOLN'S MILITARY ADVISER

ANNE CARROLL, DAUGHTER OF GOV. THOMAS K. CARROLL OF MARYLAND, CONCEIVED THE GUNBOAT STRATEGY WHICH LED TO THE CAPTURE OF FORTS DONELSON AND HENRY IN THE CIVIL WAR, AND THE ACTION WHICH WON UNION FORCES CONTROL OF THE MISSISSIPPI AND THE SUCCESSFUL SIEGE OF VICKSBURG.

IN THE CARD CATALOGUE OF THE LIBRARY OF CONGRESS, SHE IS DESCRIBED AS "THE GREAT UNRECOGNIZED MEMBER OF LINCOLN'S CABINET"

SIGN IN FAIRBANKS, ALASKA, Submitted by Dr. Ralph B. Williams, Juneau, Alaska

TOMATO PLANT 15½ FEET TALL Grown by ERSKIN COLLINS, Manassas, Va.

THE **CHURCH OF SAINT VÉRAN**, France, ORIGINALLY SERVED AS AN ANCIENT ROMAN TEMPLE OF JUPITER

A **DRUGSTORE**
IN BERGEN, NORWAY,
THE OLDEST OPERATING
BUSINESS IN THE COUNTRY..
FOUNDED 380 YEARS AGO

JEAN BAPTISTE SAHUGUET
(1713-1783)
ENTERED THE FRENCH ARMY AT THE AGE OF **7** AND
SERVED IT FOR 63 YEARS-- AT HIS DEATH HE WAS
A LIEUTENANT GENERAL

RUDOLF
SLAVITZ
(1810-1899)
OF VIENNA,
AUSTRIA,
HAD **23**
CHILDREN,
23
GRAND-
CHILDREN
AND **23**
GREAT-
GRAND-
CHILDREN

A **DRIP**
COFFEE
POT
INVENTED BY
BENJAMIN
THOMPSON, AN
AMERICAN
SCIENTIST, MORE
THAN **175**
YEARS AGO:

ST. MICHAEL'S CHAPEL NEAR CHALLES-LES-EAUX, FRANCE, HOLDS SERVICES ONLY *ONE DAY EACH YEAR*

THE **NENE GOOSE** of Hawaii, HAS WEBS BETWEEN ITS TOES ONLY HALF AS LARGE AS GEESE THAT SWIM *BECAUSE IT LIVES ITS ENTIRE LIFE ON LAVA FLOWS*

THE LAND THAT HAS NEVER HEARD OF WOMEN'S LIB

WOMEN ON THE ISLANDS OF MICRONESIA, WHEN PASSING A MAN *--BECAUSE HE IS CONSIDERED A "SUPERIOR PERSON"* -- MUST SQUAT AND SHUFFLE ALONG THE GROUND

THE **BASEMENT** OF THE CATHEDRAL OF BREMEN, GERMANY, HAS BEEN A BURIAL CRYPT FOR **460** YEARS *--YET, BODIES PLACED THERE ARE PERFECTLY PRESERVED, ALTHOUGH NOT EMBALMED*

The CATHEDRAL OF BERGEN
Norway
STILL HAS IMBEDDED IN ITS
FAÇADE A CANNONBALL FROM
A NAVAL BATTLE BETWEEN
THE DUTCH AND ENGLISH
310 YEARS AGO

ROE VAN ALSTINE of Camas, Wash.,
HAS AN AXE ONCE OWNED BY THE MOST FAMOUS OF
ALL RAIL-SPLITTERS-- *ABRAHAM LINCOLN.*
LINCOLN GAVE IT TO VAN ALSTINES GRANDFATHER IN 1860
FOR HELPING HIM SPLIT RAILS
Submitted by Emery F. Tobin,
Vancouver, Wash.

THE "SHINGLES"
OF A DOCTOR IN DORSETSHIRE,
ENGLAND, IN THE EARLY 1600's
ADVERTISES BY CARTOON
CARVINGS HIS SPECIALTIES OF
*DENTISTRY, AMPUTATION, PULSE
READING, BLOODLETTING AND
CURING BACKACHES*

THE MAUSOLEUM
NEAR LONDON, ENGLAND,
THAT HOLDS THE BODY OF
SIR RICHARD BURTON,
THE DISCOVERER OF
LAKE TANGANYIKA,
IS A MARBLE TENT

ALBERT FRANKLIN BANTA
PIONEER SETTLER OF ARIZONA,
WAS A PRINTER, POSTMASTER,
EDITOR, LEGISLATOR, SCOUT,
HISTORIAN, CONSTABLE,
DEPUTY SHERIFF, CUSTOMS
INSPECTOR, JUSTICE OF THE
PEACE, DISTRICT ATTORNEY,
PROBATE JUDGE, BROKER, LIEUT.
COLONEL AND COWBOY

MOUNT TAI-SHAN - China-
SITE OF MANY SACRED
TEMPLES, IS REACHED BY
A 5,060-FT. STAIRWAY
WITH 6,600 STEPS

THE HAMMERHEAD
HAS A CRY THAT
SOUNDS LIKE
"Take it--
Take it"

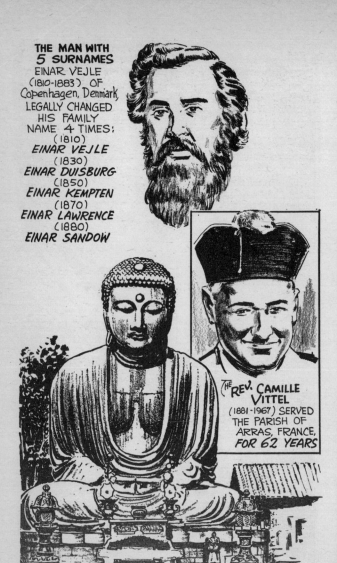

THE MAN WITH 5 SURNAMES
EINAR VEJLE (1810-1883) OF Copenhagen, Denmark, LEGALLY CHANGED HIS FAMILY NAME 4 TIMES:
(1810) *EINAR VEJLE*
(1830) *EINAR DUISBURG*
(1850) *EINAR KEMPTEN*
(1870) *EINAR LAWRENCE*
(1880) *EINAR SANDOW*

THE **REV. CAMILLE VITTEL** (1881-1967) SERVED THE PARISH OF ARRAS, FRANCE, *FOR 62 YEARS*

THE **GREAT BUDDHA** of Kamakura, Japan, 44 FEET HIGH -- HAS WITHSTOOD EARTHQUAKES, STORMS AND TIDAL WAVES FOR 723 YEARS

TRAFFIC CONGESTION ON THE STREETS OF LONDON, ENGLAND, *WAS WORSE IN 1914 THAN TODAY*

SHOES WORN BY THE NORMANS IN THE 11th CENTURY, HAD TOES SHAPED *LIKE SCORPIONS OR FISHTAILS*

MATTHEW BRADY THE CIVIL WAR PHOTOGRAPHER, MADE MANY OF HIS FAMED PHOTOS *ON WINDOW-PANES FROM SHELL-WRECKED HOUSES*

JEAN AUBERTIN (1836-1904) A CABINET-MAKER OF VITTEAUX, FRANCE, *ALWAYS SLEPT WITH ALL HIS CLOTHES ON*

MOHAMMED ALI PASHA THE VICEROY OF EGYPT, FORCED 350,000 LABORERS TO DIG A 50-MILE CANAL FROM THE ROSETTA BRANCH OF THE NILE TO ALEXANDRIA IN 1800-- *USING ONLY THEIR HANDS*

THE DRAGON KING'S CAVE
near Ichang, China, CONTAINS **3 TEMPLES,**
DEDICATED TO THE DRAGON KING

COLON T. UPDIKE OF STONE MOUNTAIN, VA., KNOWN AS "THE HUMAN HORSE," *HAD A HAIRY TAIL MORE THAN 18 INCHES LONG*

THE REV. DOROTHY M. FERRIDGE OF SOMERSET, ENGLAND, IS THE PASTOR FOR CHURCHES IN **7** VILLAGES

Submitted by
Charles H. Good
Chicago,
Ill.

101

·Oy ALKOHOLILIIKE Ab·

WHICH READS LIKE *"ALCOHOL I LIKE,"* IS FINNISH FOR **THE STATE LIQUOR AUTHORITY**

THE *"SHAKY"* **BRIDGE** OVER THE MANUHERIKIA RIVER IN Alexandra, N.Z., BUILT IN 1879, *WAS SOLD IN 1906 FOR $5*

A **BRONZE STATUE** OF NAPOLEON I IN GRENOBLE, FRANCE, SMASHED INTO BITS IN 1871 BY REVOLUTIONARIES, *WAS RECAST AS A NEW STATUE OF THE EMPEROR AT LAFFREY, FRANCE*

THE **UNICORN FISH** of Africa, HAS A HORN AND ALSO RAZOR-SHARP PROJECTIONS *ON ITS TAIL*

THE **MASCOT** OF AN INFANTRY REGIMENT IN ULM, GERMANY, WHICH FOR 19 YEARS ACCOMPANIED SENTRIES PATROLLING THE BARRACKS -- *WAS A GOOSE* (1870 -1889)

THE BELLS OF SANTA MARIA ASSUNTA IN CIELO, IN MONTECASSIANO, ITALY, TO COMMEMORATE AN EARTHQUAKE WHICH WRECKED THE BELFRY AND YET CAUSED NO LOSS OF LIFE, HAVE BEEN RUNG FOR **15** MINUTES EACH APRIL 1ST *FOR 234 YEARS*

GUILLAUME PIERRE de la MARDELLE (1752-1813) ATTORNEY GENERAL OF HAITI, BEQUEATHED 200,000 FRANCS, THE EQUIVALENT TODAY OF **$800,000,** BY A FRENCH COUNTESS FOR LEGAL WORK, REFUSED THE LEGACY SAYING *THAT WORK DONE IN FRIENDSHIP CANNOT BE VALUED IN CURRENCY*

THE FIRST CASH REGISTER LOOKED LIKE A CLOCK-- WITH ONE HAND INDICATING DOLLARS AND THE OTHER CENTS

THE EGG LAID BY A FEMALE KIWI BIRD OF NEW ZEALAND, WEIGHS ONE-SEVENTH AS MUCH AS THE ADULT BIRD HERSELF

THE IBEX CAN SCRATCH ITS BACK WITH ITS HORNS-- *WHICH GROW TO A LENGTH OF 3 FEET*

A **WILLOW TREE** ON THE ROAD BETWEEN KÖPRÜKÖY AND KIRSEHIR, TURKEY, IS A FOUNTAIN THAT GUSHES WATER *FROM ITS TRUNK FOR THIRSTY TRAVELERS*

THE **WORLD'S FOREMOST WOMEN'S LIBBERS** GIRLS OF THE SOMBA TRIBE OF DAHOMEY, AFRICA, CAN BE CLAIMED AS BRIDES ONLY AFTER THE WOULD-BE GROOM HAS WORKED FOR HER FAMILY *WITHOUT PAY FOR 8 YEARS*

THE **WHITE-COLLARED KINGFISHER** BUILDS ITS NEST IN THE WALL OF *A TERMITES' NEST*

TENNIE C. CLAFLIN AND HER SISTER, VICTORIA WOODHULL, IN 1869 FOUNDED AND SUCCESSFULLY OPERATED *WOODHULL, CLAFLIN & CO.,* THE FIRST STOCK BROKERAGE FIRM RUN BY WOMEN

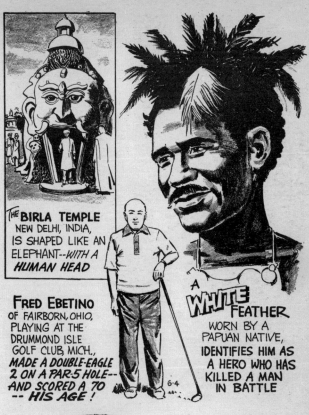

THE BIRLA TEMPLE
NEW DELHI, INDIA,
IS SHAPED LIKE AN
ELEPHANT--*WITH A
HUMAN HEAD*

FRED EBETINO
OF FAIRBORN, OHIO,
PLAYING AT THE
DRUMMOND ISLE
GOLF CLUB, MICH.,
*MADE A DOUBLE-EAGLE
2 ON A PAR-5 HOLE--
AND SCORED A 70
-- HIS AGE !*

A WHITE FEATHER
WORN BY A
PAPUAN NATIVE,
IDENTIFIES HIM AS
A HERO WHO HAS
KILLED A MAN
IN BATTLE

6-4

THE MOST ACCIDENT PRONE
MAN IN HISTORY
JOHN FOARD (1830-1910)
OF LONDON, ENGLAND
BROKE ONE OF HIS LEGS
*EVERY YEAR DURING
THE LAST 50 YEARS
OF HIS LIFE*

THE BIG BORE ERICUS AURIVILLIUS (1643-1702) PROFESSOR OF LAW AT THE UNIV. OF UPPSALA, SWEDEN, LECTURED DAILY AT THE UNIVERSITY...*YET, IN 18 YEARS, ONLY ONE STUDENT EVER ATTENDED HIS CLASS*

THE FRANCISCAN TOWER in Dubrovnik, Yugoslavia, IS DECORATED WITH THE GROTESQUE FACE OF A MASON WHO SHOWED UP FOR WORK ON ITS CONSTRUCTION INTOXICATED—
AND HE'S BEEN SHAMED FOR 700 YEARS

THE SHIP THAT BECAME AN ISLAND
A SAILING SHIP, ABANDONED IN THE MARONI RIVER BETWEEN FRENCH AND DUTCH GUIANA, FILLED WITH SOIL AND SPROUTED TREES AND PLANTS--*ALL IN A PERIOD OF 36 YEARS*

CATTLE BRED IN EGYPT 4,500 YEARS AGO, *HAD NO HORNS*

THE BEJAR BULLRING, BUILT IN 1711, *IS THE OLDEST IN ALL SPAIN*

A CHRISTIAN CHURCH
ON THE SINAI PENINSULA,
STANDS SIDE BY SIDE
WITH A MOSQUE

THE
ARETILLO
A MEXICAN
FLOWER,
RESEMBLES
AN ORNATE
EARRING

AN **ANCIENT HEADHUNTER**
OF THE SEPIK RIVER, NEW GUINEA,
STILL WEARS A HEADBAND
OF POSSUM FUR
*--TO INDICATE
HE HAS TAKEN
AT LEAST
2 HUMAN
HEADS*

ALSTON
IS THE HIGHEST MARKET
TOWN IN ALL ENGLAND

"LONDON BRIDGE"
Port Campbell, Australia,
NATURAL STONE
FORMATION

THE "KISSING" SYCAMORES
in Fifeshire, Scotland

Joë BOUSQUET
of Carcassonne, France,
BECAME ONE OF HIS
COUNTRY'S LEADING POETS AND AUTHORS--
YET HE STARTED HIS WRITING CAREER ONLY AFTER
HE HAD BEEN BEDRIDDEN BY AN ENEMY BULLET IN
WORLD WAR I ··· HE WAS AN INVALID FOR 30 YEARS,
AND WROTE 26 BOOKS

THE ROCKING STONE on Bar Harbor Pier, on Mount Desert Island, Me. HAS BEEN SHIFTED TO NEW POSITIONS BY THE WAVES —YET IT STILL RETAINS ITS *DELICATE BALANCE*

WILLIAM CUNNINGHAM A WATCHMAKER of Sanquhar, Scotland, TO WIN A BET THAT HE COULD BEAT THE LOCAL MAIL COACH, WALKED FROM GLASGOW TO SANQUHAR --A DISTANCE OF 48 MILES-- IN 8 HOURS

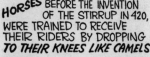

HORSES BEFORE THE INVENTION OF THE STIRRUP IN 420, WERE TRAINED TO RECEIVE THEIR RIDERS BY DROPPING *TO THEIR KNEES LIKE CAMELS*

A **STAMP** ISSUED IN SPAIN IN 1930, HONORING CHARLES LINDBERGH'S 1927 FLIGHT, INCLUDES A DRAWING *OF A BLACK CAT*

THE GROUND CUCKOO *CAN RUN AS FAST AS A RACEHORSE*

THE **ABBEY OF BAUPORT**
France,
FOR A PERIOD OF 400
YEARS, WAS THE LEGAL
OWNER OF 9 CHURCHES
IN ENGLAND

WOMEN OF THE
OASIS OF BURAYMI,
SOUTHERN ARABIA,
MUST WEAR AN
ELABORATE MASK,
WHICH GIVES THEM
THE APPEARANCE
*OF A BEAKED
BIRD OF PREY*

PEPE LLULLA
A RENOWNED
FENCING INSTRUCTOR
AND MARKSMAN
OF NEW ORLEANS, LA,
WITH A PISTOL AT
15 PACES, *SHOT AN
EGG OFF THE
HEAD OF HIS
YOUNG SON*

THE ARCH OVER THE ENTRY TO THE BIG HOUSE OF CASHEL, IRELAND, IS THE 15-FT. RIB OF A WHALE

BRACELET MONEY USED IN SWITZERLAND 3,000 YEARS AGO.

BARGE CAPTAINS ON THE ERIE CANAL, ANNOUNCED THE IMMINENT DEPARTURE OF THEIR CRAFT BY BLOWING ON A CONCH SHELL

GIRLS OF THE WA KIKUYU TRIBE OF AFRICA, HAVE THEIR EARS PIERCED IN 4 PLACES--WEARING LONG PIECES OF WOOD IN 3 HOLES DRILLED INTO THE UPPER LOBE AND A ROUND WOOD PLUG IN THE LOWER LOBE

THE BABE IN THE TREETOP A CYCLONE THAT SWEPT THROUGH MARSHFIELD, MO., LEFT AN INFANT GIRL SLEEPING PEACEFULLY IN THE BRANCHES OF A TALL ELM. *THE CHILD WAS NEVER IDENTIFIED, AND LATER WAS ADOPTED BY A LOCAL FAMILY* (April 18, 1880)

Sam TURNEY AN ATTORNEY, OF SPARTA, TENN., WHO LIKED TO EAT PAPER, WON FREEDOM FOR SEVERAL CLIENTS BY SWALLOWING VITAL DOCUMENTS *BROUGHT INTO COURT TO BE USED AGAINST THEM*

THE COFFINS USED BY NATIVES OF NEW BRITAIN, IN THE PACIFIC, *ARE BAMBOO TUBES--WHICH ARE LEFT STANDING UPRIGHT IN THE CEMETERY*

THE BOXFISH IS SO FEROCIOUS THAT WHEN SWALLOWED BY A SHARK, *IT CAN BITE ITS WAY TO FREEDOM*

THE ELEPHANT near Signes, France, *NATURAL ROCK FORMATION*

A **HERD OF GOATS** ON A NEARBY HILL, HAS FORECAST THE WEATHER FOR RADIO STATION KRSB, IN ROSEBURG, ORE. *3 TIMES EACH DAY FOR YEARS* Submitted by Jules H. Marr, Albuquerque, N.M.

WOMEN STEELWORKERS IN BHILAI, INDIA, BRING THEIR BABIES ALONG *TO EACH BUILDING SITE*

RUURLO CASTLE IN THE NETHERLANDS, HAS BEEN OCCUPIED BY THE VAN HEECKERENS FAMILY FOR **554** YEARS

THE **MOLE** HAS NOT CHANGED IN **70,000,000** YEARS

GANDA GOVINDA SINGH

(1750-1820) NATIVE MANAGER OF THE
EAST INDIA COMPANY, SPENT
$16,221,500 ON FLOWERS AND RICE
*TO BE SPRINKLED OVER
HIS MOTHER'S ASHES*

A **FENCE** on the island of Rømø, Denmark,
MADE FROM WHALE RIBS

THE CANINE CASTLE

A TOWER 75 FEET HIGH
in the Castle of Chinon,
France,
WAS ESPECIALLY BUILT
BY KING PHILIP II AS A
KENNEL FOR HIS DOGS.
*3 TREES GROWING ON
THE TOWER WERE EACH
PLANTED AS A MEMORIAL
TO A DOG THAT DIED IN
THE ROYAL KENNEL*

THE **HOMES** OF
TUNISIAN POTTERS
HAVE AT LEAST
ONE WALL
CONSISTING
OF CLAY POTS

MARY CALLINACK
A FISHWIFE OF Penzance, England, WALKED **300** MILES TO VIEW THE HYDE PARK EXPOSITION IN LONDON *AT THE AGE OF 84*
(1851)

THE **FIRST** PARACHUTIST IN HISTORY
Dr. Sebastien Lenormand
SAFELY PARACHUTED FROM THE TOWER OF THE OBSERVATORY of Montpellier, France, IN 1783
-USING A LARGE PARASOL

THE **SOVIET LEGATION** IN HELSINKI, WAS HIT BY THE FIRST BOMB DROPPED BY RUSSIAN AIRCRAFT WHEN *THEY ATTACKED FINLAND ON NOV. 30, 1939*

THE BAY of IMPERNAL Portuguese Guinea, Africa, IS 59 FEET DEEP HALF OF EACH DAY, AND DURING THE OTHER 12 HOURS, *BONE DRY*

Robert GREVILLE, Lord Brooke
1607-1643
WHO BOMBARDED THE CATHEDRAL OF LICHFIELD, ENGLAND, TO RUBBLE, ASSURED HIS SHOCKED TROOPS THAT THE ACT WOULD BE ACKNOWLEDGED **BY A SIGN FROM HEAVEN** -- *THE EDIFICE, KNOWN AS ST. CHAD'S CATHEDRAL, WAS DESTROYED ON ST. CHAD'S DAY - AND A FEW MOMENTS LATER LORD BROOKE WAS KILLED INSTANTLY BY A BULLET THAT PIERCED ONE OF HIS EYES!*

OPTICAL ILLUSION DRAWN WITH ONE LINE

Stone Hearts WERE PLACED BY BRITONS **2,000** YEARS AGO *IN THE GRAVES OF MISERS*

THE FIRST SPORTS TROPHY A COPPER CUP, DEPICTING 2 WRESTLERS, FOUND IN IRAQ IN 1938, IS MORE THAN **4,700** YEARS OLD

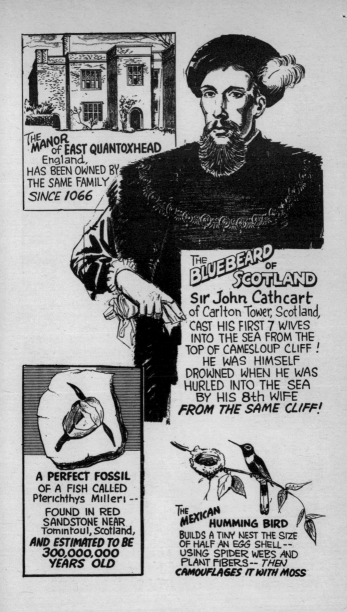

THE MANOR of **EAST QUANTOXHEAD** England, HAS BEEN OWNED BY THE SAME FAMILY *SINCE 1066*

THE **BLUEBEARD** of **SCOTLAND**
SIR John Cathcart
of Carlton Tower, Scotland, CAST HIS FIRST 7 WIVES INTO THE SEA FROM THE TOP OF CAMESLOUP CLIFF! HE WAS HIMSELF DROWNED WHEN HE WAS HURLED INTO THE SEA BY HIS 8th WIFE *FROM THE SAME CLIFF!*

A PERFECT FOSSIL OF A FISH CALLED Pterichthys Milleri -- FOUND IN RED SANDSTONE NEAR Tomintoul, Scotland, *AND ESTIMATED TO BE* **300,000,000 YEARS OLD**

THE **MEXICAN HUMMING BIRD** BUILDS A TINY NEST THE SIZE OF HALF AN EGG SHELL -- USING SPIDER WEBS AND PLANT FIBERS -- *THEN CAMOUFLAGES IT WITH MOSS*

A PILLAR OF SALT
ON THE SHORE OF THE DEAD SEA, THAT IS POINTED OUT BY NATIVES AS **LOT'S WIFE**

COLONEL
SIR WILLIAM HUDDLESTON
(1603-1668)
WAS ONE OF **9** BROTHERS
-ALL OF WHOM SERVED AS
COLONELS IN THE ARMY OF
KING CHARLES I DURING
THE ENGLISH CIVIL WAR

THE HAND
A MEXICAN
FLOWER WITH
5 STAMENS
RESEMBLES
A HAND,
EVEN TO THE
FINGERNAILS

BENJAMIN SCHULZE (1689-1760) COPIED THE BIBLE IN LONGHAND 3 TIMES--*EACH TIME IN A DIFFERENT HINDU LANGUAGE.* HE KNEW 100 FOREIGN ALPHABETS, AND COULD RECITE THE LORD'S PRAYER IN 215 LANGUAGES

THE **CAPE** TURTLE DOVE OF SOUTH AFRICA, HAS A CRY THAT SOUNDS LIKE *"TELL FATHER, TELL FATHER."*

THE **DEFENSE TOWER** OF NEUWERK ISLAND, NEAR CUXHAVEN, GERMANY, HAS WALLS *10 FEET THICK*

GETA (189-212) Emperor of Rome INSISTED UPON **ALLITERATIVE MEALS**

A TYPICAL MENU:
PERDIX (PARTRIDGE) PERSICA (PEACH)
PAVO (PEACOCK) PRUNA (PLUM)
PORRUM (LEEK) PEPONE (MELON)
PHASEOLI (BEANS)

ALL IN THE FAMILY
3 BROTHERS AND 2 SISTERS OF THE ESCE FAMILY OF SYRACUSE, N.Y. **MARRIED 3 SISTERS AND 2 BROTHERS** OF THE GARZIO FAMILY
Submitted by Mrs. Anthony Ross of Liverpool, N.Y. – (*A daughter of one of the couples*)

THE **LITTLE BLACKBIRD** OF THE ISLES

CAN BE FOUND ONLY ON THE TINY ISLAND OF COUSIN, IN THE INDIAN OCEAN

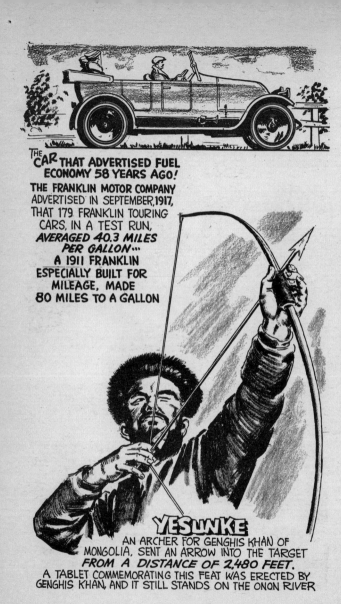

THE CAR THAT ADVERTISED FUEL ECONOMY 58 YEARS AGO!

THE FRANKLIN MOTOR COMPANY ADVERTISED IN SEPTEMBER, 1917, THAT 179 FRANKLIN TOURING CARS, IN A TEST RUN, *AVERAGED 40.3 MILES PER GALLON*... A 1911 FRANKLIN ESPECIALLY BUILT FOR MILEAGE, MADE 80 MILES TO A GALLON

YESUNKE

AN ARCHER FOR GENGHIS KHAN OF MONGOLIA, SENT AN ARROW INTO THE TARGET *FROM A DISTANCE OF 2,480 FEET.* A TABLET COMMEMORATING THIS FEAT WAS ERECTED BY GENGHIS KHAN, AND IT STILL STANDS ON THE ONON RIVER

NOSU WOMEN OF CHINA, CREATE GIGANTIC HEADDRESSES BY WEAVING INTO THEIR HAIR *QUANTITIES OF DYED WOOL*

COUNT VERIER A FRENCHMAN, IN AN EXHIBITION AT THE SARATOGA, N.Y., RACES IN 1880, PLACED AN APPLE ON THE BARE HEAD OF A FRIEND, AND THEN LEAPED HIS HORSE OVER A HURDLE AND *SLICED THE APPLE IN HALF WITH HIS SABER WHILE IN MIDAIR*

2-7

THE **MALA PANDARAMS** of Kerala, India, ARE ONE OF THE FEW PEOPLE ON EARTH WHO NEVER BUILD HOMES -- *PREFERRING TO LIVE IN HOLLOW TREES OR UNDER ROCK LEDGES*

A **MEMORIAL** in Lincoln, Nebraska, TO THE NEBRASKAN INDIANS, DEPICTS AN INDIAN SENDING A SMOKE SIGNAL -- *A WARNING OF THE APPROACH OF THE WHITE MAN*

NICHOLAS ZOGRAPHOS (1886 - 1953) A PROFESSIONAL GAMBLER, LEFT AN ESTATE OF **$14,000,000** EVERY DOLLAR OF IT WON PLAYING BACCARAT

JOSEPH JUSTUS SCALIGER (1540-1609) GREATEST SCHOLAR OF HIS TIME, *ALWAYS BECAME HYSTERICAL AT THE SIGHT OF WATERCRESS*

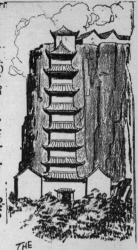

THE **STRANGEST STAIRWAY IN THE WORLD**

A BUDDHIST TEMPLE BUILT ON SHIH-PAO-CHAI ROCK NEAR CHONGCHOW, CHINA, CAN BE REACHED ONLY BY CLIMBING **200** FEET UP *THE SIDE OF A 9-STORY PAGODA*

THE **STATUE** OF QUEEN INES de CASTRO of Portugal, THAT ADORNS HER GRAVE in Alcobaca, Portugal, SHOWS HER WEARING ONLY ONE GLOVE *-BECAUSE IN LIFE SHE ALWAYS WORE ONE GLOVE AND CARRIED THE OTHER*

A **COAL MINE** near Neunkirchen, Saar, Germany, *LOCATED ABOVE THE GROUND*

The letters on the building read: **PARRAISON** and **TOUT**

THE **GATEWAY** TO THE CITY OF Poitiers, France, IS SURMOUNTED BY 13 CHIMNEYS --EACH INSCRIBED WITH A SINGLE LETTER-- BUT READ CONSECUTIVELY THEY SPELL THE PHRASE "**TOUT PAR RAISON**" *TRANSLATED FREELY IT CONVEYS THE 16th CENTURY CITY FATHERS' MESSAGE THAT "EVERYTHING HAS A REASON"*

ROBERT FARRIES A SCHOOL-MASTER IN NEW ABBEY, Scotland, WORE NO CLOTHING EXCEPT THAT WHICH HE HAD *TAKEN FROM SCARE-CROWS* (from (1781-1806)

THE **PIG-MOUTH MONEY OF SIAM** STANDARD UNITS OF SILVER CURRENCY -14th Century-

NATIVE HOMES in Papua ARE CREATED IN THE SHAPE OF THE OPEN MOUTH OF A CROCODILE *-IN THE BELIEF THIS WILL MAKE THE FIERCE REPTILES ACT FRIENDLIER TOWARD THE OCCUPANTS*

AN **ENSIGN** THE LOWEST COMMISSIONED RANK IN THE ROYAL MUSKETEERS OF FRANCE, GOT HIS COMMISSION IN THE 17th CENTURY BY *PAYING $ 39,000*

THE **HÜWEN MILL** in Germany, IS POWERED BY BOTH *WIND AND WATER*

JACQUES ANTOINE MOERENHOUT (1769-1879) ALTHOUGH A CITIZEN OF BELGIUM, SUCCESSIVELY SERVED IN TAHITI AS *THE AMERICAN CONSUL AND AS THE FRENCH CONSUL*

MESSAGES ETCHED BY ESKIMOS *ON THE JAWBONES OF WHALES*

Samuel **CHAPELL** 1792-1880 of London, England, DURING HIS ENTIRE LIFETIME **NEVER ATE SOLID FOOD !** *HE CARRIED A GRATER WITH HIM ALWAYS*

THE **CANDELABRA PALM** AN ARECA PALM ON THE ISLAND OF BOURBON, IN THE INDIAN OCEAN

THE **AQUEDUCT of TARRAGONA**, Spain, 88 FT. HIGH AND 712 FT. LONG, WAS BUILT WITHOUT MORTAR--*YET IT HAS ENDURED FOR 1,900 YEARS*

THE **JERBOA** GATHERS DRY GRASS, TWISTS IT INTO A SHEAF AND CARRIES IT IN THE CURVE OF ITS TAIL TO WHERE IT WEAVES ITS NEST

THE **LEAF CATFISH** OF THE AMAZON, LOOKS MORE LIKE A LEAF THAN A FISH

126

"AMBITION," IN LATIN, ORIGINALLY MEANT "WALKING ABOUT TO SOLICIT VOTES"

BEDOUINS OF THE ALGERIAN SAHARA, OFTEN SLEEP ON THE BACKS OF WALKING CAMELS

STUFFED CROCODILES WERE HUNG OVER DOORWAYS IN Wadi-el-Arab, Nubia, Africa, TO FRIGHTEN AWAY *EVIL SPIRITS*

SABBATH BONNETS RESEMBLING THOSE WORN BY THE WIVES OF MISSIONARIES WERE MADE BY NATIVES OF THE NEW HEBRIDES OUT OF TURTLE SHELL

ONLY ONE SILVER ECU, A COIN WORTH ABOUT 58 CENTS, *WAS EVER MINTED BY CORSICA* (1736)

THE CEMETERY ARCH THAT SEEMS TO WEEP
Cedar Grove Cemetery, New Bern, N.C.
THE ARCH IS MADE OF COQUINA SHELLS
- FROM WHICH MOISTURE DRIPS CONSTANTLY
LIKE TEARDROPS

GEORGE EDMUND STREET (1824-1881)
FAMED ENGLISH ARCHITECT-
WON A CONTEST TO DESIGN THE
ROYAL COURTS OF JUSTICE IN
LONDON, IN 1868
*-BUT DIED OF EXHAUSTION
AFTER DRAWING 3,000
SUCCESSIVE PLANS FOR
THE STRUCTURES*

THE **NEST** OF THE **TAILOR-BIRD** of India,
IS MADE FROM A SINGLE LEAF.
IT IS LACED TOGETHER WITH VEGETABLE FIBER BY THE BIRD

THE **THOROUGHFARE** IN SAN JUAN, PUERTO RICO, THAT LINKS **ATLANTIC PL.** AND **PACIFIC PL.**, IS NAMED *PANAMA CANAL*

GRAVES in Sierra Leone, Africa, HAVE A THATCHED ROOF-- *TO MAKE THE SPIRITS FEEL AT HOME*

INFLATION in the 12TH CENTURY
The **CHATEAU de VOUFFLENS** in Switzerland, WAS EXCHANGED BY GUILLELME de WOLFLENS *FOR A NEW COAT FOR HIS WIFE* (1175)

RAJWAR of Gurapur, India, WAS A WIFE FOR ONE DAY-- *AND A WIDOW FOR 70 YEARS*

A **RAINCOAT AND HAT** MADE BY AN ESKIMO FROM A SEAL'S INTESTINES

The **CRADLE** BUILT FOR KING HENRY V IN 1387, WAS ADORNED WITH 2 WOODEN BIRDS WHICH WHISTLED A LULLABY WHEN **THE CRADLE WAS ROCKED.** *IT IS STILL PRESERVED AT MONMOUTH CASTLE, England*

FRANÇOIS QUESNEL (1765-1819)
SERVED AS A GENERAL IN THE
ARMIES OF **FRANCE, ITALY, THE
NETHERLANDS AND SPAIN**

THE **EVIL EYE**
IS KEPT FROM WEDDINGS
AMONG THE MADIGAS of India,
BY THE SACRIFICE OF A GOAT
-- WITH THE KNIFE WIELDER
*LEAVING BLOODY PALM
PRINTS ON A WALL TO
FRIGHTEN OFF THE SPIRITS*

**WEAVER
BIRDS**
OF AFRICA,
BUILD THEIR
NESTS BY
WEAVING STRIPS
OF GRASS-- *WITH
ONE BIRD OUTSIDE AND THE
OTHER POKING BACK THE STRIPS
FROM INSIDE THE NEST* ...

**PHOENICIAN
BOTTLE**
COLORED VIOLET,
BROWN AND PURPLE-
MADE 2,400 YEARS
AGO BY WINDING A
CONTINUOUS STRIP
OF OPAQUE GLASS

THE **UPSIDE-DOWN
CATFISH**
SWIMS AND FEEDS
UPSIDE DOWN

THE ANCIENT THEATER
IN VAISON-LA-ROMAINE, FRANCE,
IS THE ONLY ROMAN THEATER
RUIN IN THE WORLD THAT
*STILL HAS ITS ENTRANCE
COLUMNS INTACT*

DR. JOHN LEYDEN (1775-1811)
MASTERED 45 FOREIGN
LANGUAGES -- OF WHICH
28 WERE ORIENTAL

THE **WORLD'S
RAREST BIRD**
THE MAURITIUS
KESTREL, A TINY
HAWKLIKE BIRD,
IS FOUND ONLY
IN MAURITIUS IN
THE INDIAN OCEAN,
*--AND THERE ARE
ONLY **7** OF THEM*

SCOUT BEES
INFORM THE REST
OF THE HIVE OF
THE DISTANCE AND
DIRECTION OF A
NEW NESTING PLACE
*BY PERFORMING A
WAGGLE DANCE*

THE **BLACKTHORN
TREE** at Bra,
Italy, HAS BURST
INTO BLOOM ON
THE COLDEST
DAY OF WINTER
ANNUALLY FOR
**639
YEARS**

THE **LEANING TOWER OF KITZINGEN**
Germany
–WHEN YOU WALK AROUND IT–
APPEARS TO TILT IN DIFFERENT DIRECTIONS

THE **OPENHEARTED MAN!**
HUGH, 3d Viscount.
Montgomery County Down,
Ireland, AS THE RESULT OF A
CHILDHOOD INJURY, HAD AN
OPENING IN HIS LEFT SIDE
THROUGH WHICH HIS
*PULSATING HEART WAS
CLEARLY VISIBLE*

A **GOLDEN CALENDAR**
WAS PART OF THE
CORONATION REGALIA
OF KING CHARLES X
OF FRANCE--
SYMBOLIZING THAT
HE WAS THE
SUPREME MASTER
OF TIME

Don
Francisco
Antonio **ZEA** (1770-1822)
WAS PROFESSOR OF NATURAL
HISTORY AT THE UNIVERSITY
OF BOGOTÁ, COLOMBIA,
AT THE AGE OF 16

THE CHANCEL
OF THE CHURCH OF ST. MARTIN,
IN PFAFFENHEIM, FRANCE,
WAS BUILT IN 1230 -- BUT THE
REST OF THE EDIFICE WAS
*CONSTRUCTED 668 YEARS
LATER*

KAYA-KAYA WOMEN
of New Guinea,
WEAR A HAIRDO IN WHICH
*IS BRAIDED 30 POUNDS
OF OIL-SOAKED GRASS*

A
*BIRD'S
NEST* OF **4** STORIES,
BUILT BY A YELLOW
WARBLER ATTEMPTING
TO THWART THE
INTRUSIONS OF A
COWBIRD THAT
WANTED THE WARBLER
*TO HATCH THE
COWBIRD'S EGGS*

THE LILY-LEAF CATERPILLAR
MAKES A CLOAK FOR
ITSELF BY BITING OFF
2 PIECES OF A LILY PAD
AND STITCHING THEM
AROUND ITS BODY
WITH STRANDS OF SILK

THE CRATER GAME PRESERVE

NGORONGORO, A VOLCANIC CRATER IN THE CONGO, IS 12 MILES IN DIAMETER, 35 MILES IN CIRCUMFERENCE, 2,000' DEEP--AND CONTAINS 75,000 HEAD OF BIG GAME WHICH NEVER LEAVE IT

JOHN RAWLINGS
of Lower Portwood, England, NAMED HIS **3 DAUGHTERS** Hope, Faith and Charity-- AND HIS **3 SONS,** Justice, Morality and Fortitude

A **WIDOW** IN SARDINIA, ITALY, MUST REMAIN INSIDE HER HOME CONTINUOUSLY FOR *A PERIOD OF AT LEAST 3 YEARS*

THE KORNATI ISLANDS
IN YUGOSLAVIA,
COMPRISE 125 SMALL
ISLANDS--NO **2** OF WHICH
HAVE THE SAME SHAPE

**THE WOMEN WHO
ARE KEPT UNDER
LOCK AND KEY!**

WOMEN of Niamey,
Africa,
MUST WEAR SILVER
PADLOCKS--WHICH HANG
FROM THEIR NOSES AND
OVER THEIR MOUTHS

FATHER OF THE WEEK!
Jacques Semaine
(1871-1912) of Paris, France,
WHOSE LAST NAME IN
FRENCH MEANS "WEEK", WAS
THE FATHER OF 7 CHILDREN--
*GUILLAUME, BORN ON SUNDAY
PIERRE, BORN ON MONDAY
FERNANDE, BORN ON TUESDAY
AMANDE, BORN ON WEDNESDAY
ROBERT, BORN ON THURSDAY
JOSEPH, BORN ON FRIDAY
AND STANISLAS,
BORN ON SATURDAY*

REST, IN JAPANESE SCRIPT, IS SIGNIFIED BY THE CHARACTER FOR "MAN" 亻 PLACED AGAINST THAT FOR A "TREE" 木

ROCHECORBON CLIFF near Tours, France, IS A NATURAL SKY-SCRAPER APARTMENT HOUSE-- THE HOME FOR WINE MAKERS WHO HAVE *BUILT 3 STORIES OF DWELLINGS IN THE ROCK*

NATIVES OF THE BUCCANEER ARCHIPELAGO, AUSTRALIA, GO TO SEA ON SMALL RAFTS OF MANGROVE LOGS-- *ON WHICH THEY STAND*

MOUNT SAANA FORMS A BORDER BETWEEN *FINLAND, SWEDEN AND NORWAY*

THE **SCYTHE TREE**
Waterloo, N.Y.,
A BALM OF GILEAD THAT
HAS GROWN AROUND **3**
SCYTHES--EACH LEFT IN
THE TREE'S CROTCH BY
*MEN WHO WENT OFF
TO WARS OVER A PERIOD
OF 57 YEARS*
Submitted by Emery F. Tobin,
Vancouver, Wash.

THE **FAMED
FAREWELL ADDRESS**
OF GEORGE WASHINGTON
WAS ACTUALLY WRITTEN,
EXCEPT FOR MINOR CHANGES,
BY ALEXANDER HAMILTON

ROBERT C. GRIER
(1794-1870) A JUSTICE OF
THE U.S. SUPREME COURT,
READ A CHAPTER OF THE
NEW TESTAMENT FIRST IN
GREEK AND THEN IN ENGLISH
*EVERY WEEK OF
HIS ADULT LIFE...*
FROM THE AGE OF 18 HE READ
THE NEW TESTAMENT FROM
COVER TO COVER **10 TIMES**

WOMEN'S LIB IN THE FAR EAST
LAI CHOI SAN, A NOTORIOUS WOMAN PIRATE OF BIAS BAY, CHINA, OPERATED 12 ARMED JUNKS; WAS ACCOMPANIED EVERYWHERE BY BODYGUARDS-- *AND WAS NEVER CAPTURED*

12 TOWER HOMES WERE CONSTRUCTED IN ALBENGA, ITALY, IN 1096, UNDER A SPECIAL DISPENSATION GRANTED TO RESIDENTS WHO *MANNED THEIR OWN WARSHIPS IN THE FIRST CRUSADE*

A **CRUISER** HURLED ONTO THE BEACH AT Westport Point, Mass., IN THE NEW ENGLAND HURRICANE OF 1954, *WAS NAMED "LAST FLING"*

THE **UNFINISHED TOWER**
Malines, Belgium,
THE SPIRE WAS PLANNED TO RISE **548** FEET, BUT CONSTRUCTION WAS HALTED AT **318** FEET FOR LACK OF FUNDS AND IT HAS REMAINED UNCOMPLETED FOR **600 YEARS**

CHIEF JUSTICE WILLIAM CUSHING
1732-1810
of the U.S. Supreme Court
WAS THE LAST AMERICAN JURIST TO WEAR THE *FULL WIG OF AN ENGLISH JUDGE*

THE **RESIN GNAT**
ALWAYS BUILDS ITS NEST ON A LUMP OF RESIN ON A PINE TREE

THE **STRUCTURE** HOUSING ARGENTINA'S CONGRESS IN BUENOS AIRES, *IS A COPY OF THE U.S. CAPITOL*

BARON ANTON ZACH
(1747-1826)
JOINED THE AUSTRIAN ARMY AS A LIEUTENANT IN 1764 AND RETIRED AS A FIELD MARSHAL *AFTER SERVING 61 YEARS*

A **PALM TREE** in Elche, Spain, THAT ACTUALLY IS 7 DIFFERENT TREES WHICH GREW FROM THE TRUNK OF A PALM 80 YEARS AGO, AFTER THE TRUNK WAS 70 YEARS OLD

THE TEMPLE OF MARTAND - Kashmir.
NOW ONLY A RUIN, WAS BUILT WITH 84 COLUMNS BECAUSE 84 IS A SACRED NUMBER IN INDIA--
THE PRODUCT OF THE NUMBER OF DAYS IN THE WEEK TIMES THE NUMBER OF MONTHS IN THE YEAR

THE ALADJA MONASTERY
at Slantchev Brjag, Bulgaria, WAS BUILT IN THE 6th CENTURY *INSIDE A ROCKY MOUNTAIN*

NATURE'S JIGSAW PUZZLE PIECES OF BARK SHED BY PONDEROSA TREES FIT INTO EACH OTHER LIKE JIGSAW PIECES - SOME FORM THE SHAPES OF BIRDS AND ANIMALS

Submitted by Millard Cox, Los Alamos, N.M.

AG MUHAMAD el HADDAD WAS ELECTED KING OF TRIPOLI SOLELY BECAUSE HE WAS THAT COUNTRY'S *ONLY BLOND SOLDIER*... HE RULED FROM 1673 TO 1679

THE GUARDIAN MONSTERS
WARARIKI BEACH, SO. ISLAND, N.Z., NATURAL ROCK FORMATION

THE **PAGANI THEATER** IN MONTERUBBIANO, ITALY, WAS STARTED BY BRUNO PAGANI AS HIS PALACE, BUT HIS SUDDEN DEATH LEFT IT UNFINISHED FOR 279 YEARS - *--UNTIL IT WAS COMPLETED IN 1862 AS A THEATER*

DR. CHARLES V. RILEY
(1843-1895)
the famed American entomologist PLAGUED BY INSOMNIA, COULD ONLY SLEEP ON A MOVING TRAIN OR IN A BARBER'S CHAIR

THE MAN WHO BACKED HIS THEORY WITH HIS LIFE!
Tancredo Lopez — A SPANISH BULLFIGHTER DRESSED COMPLETELY IN WHITE AND PERMITTED A BULL TO CHARGE AT HIM TO TEST HIS BELIEF THAT A BULL WILL NOT ATTACK AN IMMOBILE OBJECT THE BULL STOPPED JUST SHORT OF GORING HIM

SIAMESE CATS IN THAILAND, WERE CONSIDERED SACRED AND COULD BE OWNED *ONLY BY THOSE OF ROYAL BLOOD*

THE GREAT ROWBOATS of the Kavirondo, Africa, WHICH CARRY 20 TO 40 OARSMEN, ARE CONSTRUCTED OF BOARDS SEWN TOGETHER *WITH FIBER ROPE*

THE "ROLLER COASTER" BRIDGE OVER THE DALÄLVEN RIVER, AT ÖSTERFORS, SWEDEN, *FLOATS ON THE WATER*

A PORKPIE HAT WORN BY A WOMAN IN EVOLÈNE, FRANCE, INDICATES ITS WEARER *IS MARRIED*

THE MASON BEE
BUILDS FOR EACH OF HER EGGS AN INDIVIDUAL CELL OF CLAY AND SAND, WHICH IS STOCKED WITH POLLEN AND HONEY

John White GEARY (1819-1873)
THE FIRST AMERICAN MAYOR OF SAN FRANCISCO, ALSO SERVED AS *GOVERNOR* OF *KANSAS,* *GOVERNOR* OF *PENNSYLVANIA,* *MILITARY GOVERNOR* OF *SAVANNAH, GA.--* AND WAS *OFFERED THE GOVERNORSHIP OF UTAH, BUT DECLINED*

LYMAN BEECHER
(1775-1863) CONGREGATIONAL MINISTER AND FATHER OF HARRIET BEECHER STOWE, WAS THE FATHER OF **7 CONGREGATIONAL MINISTERS**

MAGIC FLUTES
USED BY ALL TIBETAN MAGICIANS, MUST BE MADE FROM THE THIGH BONE OF *A GIRL OF NOBLE BIRTH WHO DIED AT THE AGE OF 16*

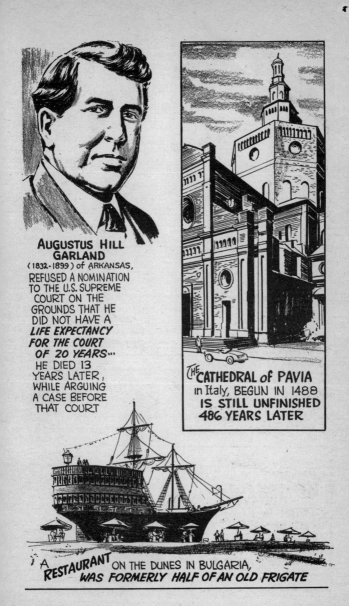

AUGUSTUS HILL GARLAND (1832-1899) of ARKANSAS, REFUSED A NOMINATION TO THE U.S. SUPREME COURT ON THE GROUNDS THAT HE DID NOT HAVE A *LIFE EXPECTANCY FOR THE COURT OF 20 YEARS*... HE DIED 13 YEARS LATER, WHILE ARGUING A CASE BEFORE THAT COURT

THE **CATHEDRAL of PAVIA** in Italy, BEGUN IN 1488 **IS STILL UNFINISHED 486 YEARS LATER**

A **RESTAURANT** ON THE DUNES IN BULGARIA, *WAS FORMERLY HALF OF AN OLD FRIGATE*

THE **GREAT CUP** NEAR THE CATHEDRAL OF SPEYER, GERMANY, WAS ONCE A SANCTUARY WHICH ASSURED IMMUNITY TO ANY CRIMINAL *WHO HAD CLIMBED INTO THE CUP*

THE **FIREPROOFED MAN** A **NATIVE** of Kondoa, Africa, BY APPLYING A VEGETABLE JUICE TO HIS SKIN, CAN HOLD A *FLAMING TORCH TO HIS BARE CHEST*

THE TOWN COUNCIL BUILDING IN BRISTOL, ENGLAND, SINCE 1500 HAS SERVED AS *A PRIVATE HOME, A SUGAR REFINERY, A ROYAL MINT AND A HOME FOR PAUPERS*

A **WHITE MARBLE GRIZZLY BEAR** CARVED BY TLINGIT INDIANS OF ALASKA AS A **GRAVE MARKER** Submitted by Emery F. Tobin, Vancouver, Wash.

BIRD'S NEST FUNGUS IS SHAPED LIKE A CUP --*AND INSIDE IT ARE ROUND WHITE PELLETS THAT LOOK LIKE BIRDS' EGGS*

A **HEADDRESS** WORN BY A NATIVE OF NEW GUINEA, FASHIONED OF HAIR AND DRIED GRASS TO PROTECT THE BACK OF THE NECK *FROM ENEMY CLUBS*

THE **TEMPLE** IN THE PARK OF THE IMPERIAL SUMMER PALACE IN Jehol, China, *IS MADE OF SOLID COPPER*

THE **GRASS TREES** OF AUSTRALIA, GROW AT THE RATE OF ONE FOOT EVERY **120 YEARS**

THE CHAPEL of ST. MARTIN IN CALFEISENTAL, AUSTRIA, SERVED A CONGREGATION FOR **400** YEARS BUT HAS *BEEN ABANDONED SINCE 1600*

A
UNICORN RAM
EXHIBITED IN
ENGLAND IN 1790

STOVES
IN MOMBASA,
KENYA, ARE
MADE OUT OF
ELEPHANTS'
FEET

THE FIRST DEMOCRACIES
VILLAGES IN INDIA, ELECTED A
GOVERNING BOARD OF 5 MEN TO
ADMINISTER THEIR AFFAIRS,
*FOR A PERIOD OF
4,500 YEARS*

SCHOOLCHILDREN
in Japan,
OFTEN ATTEND CLASSES WITH
A YOUNGER BROTHER OR
SISTER **ON THEIR BACK**

GINERY TWITCHELL
(1811-1883)
A MAIL RIDER, TRAVELED BY HORSEBACK FROM WORCESTER, MASS, TO HARTFORD, CONN., A DISTANCE OF **60 MILES, IN 3 HOURS AND 20 MINUTES**-- *THROUGH SNOW 2 FEET DEEP !* Jan. 23, 1846

AN ANCIENT LINDEN TREE in Bordesholm, Germany, FOR 200 YEARS, SHADED SESSIONS OF A COURT KNOWN AS **THE LINDEN TRIBUNAL**

CHILDREN of New Guinea, ARE INVARIABLY BLOND -- *YET AS THEY GROW OLDER, THEY ALWAYS BECOME DARK HAIRED*

TABLE MOUNTAIN
IN CAPE TOWN, SO. AFRICA, IS USUALLY COVERED WITH A FLEECY WHITE CLOUD WHICH IS KNOWN AS *THE TABLECLOTH*

THE **REV. JOHN RUSSELL** (1795-1883) of Exeter, England, SERVED SUCCESSIVELY IN **3** PARISHES -- *A TOTAL OF* **64** *YEARS*

THE **MOUNTAIN GOAT** IS NOT A GOAT-- *IT IS AKIN TO THE ANTELOPE*

THE **CHURCH** of **SAN GIUSTA** NEAR ORISTANO, ITALY, WAS BUILT IN THE 13th CENTURY FROM *THE BUILDING STONES OF AN ANCIENT ROMAN TEMPLE*

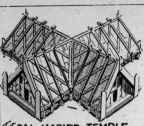

THE **PAI MARIRE TEMPLE** IN WAITAKI, NEW ZEALAND, A WOODEN STRUCTURE IN THE SHAPE OF A CROSS, WAS BUILT BY THE MAORIS IN 1863 WITHOUT THE USE OF NAILS OR IRON BRACES --YET IT HAS ENDURED FOR 112 YEARS

A **LLAMA** TURNED LOOSE BY A BANKRUPT CIRCUS, ROAMED THE STREETS OF MANAOS, BRAZIL, FOR MONTHS

SUITS THAT NEVER NEED PRESSING
MEN OF NOBLE BIRTH ON IFALIK ISLAND, TATTOO THEIR BODIES TO RESEMBLE CLOTHING-- *USING FISHBONE OR BAMBOO NEEDLES*

THE **MOST POPULAR DESSERT** AT ALL BANQUETS IN ANCIENT ROME *WAS A SWEET ONION*

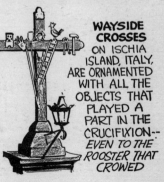

WAYSIDE CROSSES ON ISCHIA ISLAND, ITALY, ARE ORNAMENTED WITH ALL THE OBJECTS THAT PLAYED A PART IN THE CRUCIFIXION-- *EVEN TO THE ROOSTER THAT CROWED*

A **RESTAURANT** IN KYOTO, JAPAN, LOCATED IN AN OLD WATER MILL

THE MINUET
ANTHILLS IN THE NORTHERN ROPE RIVER TERR. OF AUSTRALIA THAT *LOOK LIKE 2 DANCING WOMEN*

ANOTHER WIN FOR WOMEN'S LIB!
Mrs. Betty Egan *IS FIRE MARSHAL* FOR THE TESUQUE, NEW MEXICO FIRE DISTRICT
Submitted by Jules H. Marr, Albuquerque, N.M.

THE **PREHISTORIC BIRD**
NATURAL ROCK FORMATION
The Arch of Abu Maghrur, Riyadh, Saudi Arabia

THE SQUARE TOWER AT THE EDGE OF THE OLD ROMAN MEAT MARKET, IS THE MOST ANCIENT STRUCTURE IN ALL VIENNA--**HAVING SERVED AS A FORTIFICATION 1,800 YEARS AGO**

THE FIRST "SEX CHANGE" Helen Barkoczy (1833-1900) THE ONLY DESCENDANT OF THE IMMENSELY WEALTHY COUNT JOHN BARKOCZY, *WAS LEGALLY DECLARED A MAN IN 1871, SO SHE COULD INHERIT HIS ESTATE*

THE BRIDGE OF STENNÄSET Sweden, WITH 2 ARCHES 20 FEET HIGH, WAS BUILT OF STONES WITHOUT THE USE OF MORTAR-- *YET IT HAS ENDURED FOR 179 YEARS*

THE OLDEST SCULPTURED MONUMENT IN EUROPE
THE LION GATE IN MYCENAE, GREECE, IS **3,325 YEARS OLD**

MONKS
IN THE HERMIT MONASTERY OF KETHO, TIBET, ALTERNATE BETWEEN **3** YEARS, **3** MONTHS AND **13** DAYS OF OUTSIDE FREEDOM-- AND **3 YEARS, 3 MONTHS AND 13 DAYS** OF SOLITARY CONFINEMENT IN A MEDITATION CELL

THE **TOWER OF HERCULES** IN CORUÑA, SPAIN, HAS BEEN USED AS A LIGHTHOUSE *CONTINUOUSLY FOR MORE THAN 1,800 YEARS* THE ROMANS ORIGINALLY KEPT AN OIL FIRE BURNING ON IT

THE **HARLEQUIN BEETLE** OF CAYENNE, FRENCH GUIANA, HAS FORELEGS *TWICE AS LONG AS ITS BODY*

3 BRIDGES near Ponthaut, France, CONSTRUCTED ONE ABOVE ANOTHER

BOYS OF THE AKHA TRIBE OF CHINA, *ARE ALL PIPE SMOKERS*

ELLEN CHURCH A REGISTERED NURSE FROM SAN FRANCISCO, CALIF., WAS THE WORLD'S FIRST AIR STEWARDESS
- May 15, 1930 -

WET CLUMPS FROM THE SWAMPS OF PETSAMO, IN RUSSIAN FINLAND, ARE DUG UP AND LEFT ON SPEARS *IN AN ATTEMPT BY THE NATIVES TO DRY OUT THE SWAMPS*

THE COW TREE IN SO. AMERICA, WHEN TAPPED, EMITS A STREAM OF WHITE SAP *THAT HAS MANY OF THE QUALITIES OF MILK*

THE **TEMPLE OF MATS** ON SACRED ISLAND, JAPAN, IS DECORATED WITH *HUNDREDS OF WOODEN RICE SPOONS*

St. SWITHUN'S CHURCH in Winchester, England *WAS BUILT OVER THE CITY GATE*

A JET PLANE PASSING THRU THE SOUND BARRIER AT PULIGNY-MONTRACHET, FRANCE, TOUCHED OFF A SONIC BOOM *THAT SHATTERED 3,000 BOTTLES OF FINE WINE*

SACRE BLEU!

THE ANCIENT THEATER
IN PERGAMUM, TURKEY,
THE STEEPEST GRECO-ROMAN
THEATER IN THE WORLD,
HAS SEATS BUILT INTO
THE SIDE OF A
MOUNTAIN--**165 FEET**
ABOVE THE STAGE

THE
EXPLORER
NATURAL ROCK
FORMATION
-- DISCOVERED IN THE
ANTARCTIC IN 1910,
BY MEMBERS OF THE
SCOTT EXPEDITION

THE **KREMLIN** IN MOSCOW,
CONTAINS **7** CHURCHES
--*ALL NOW PUT TO OTHER USES*

THE
TAILED VIEJAS
of So. America,
HATCHES ITS EGGS IN
A CAVITY UNDER
ITS LOWER JAW

157

ANTHONY L. GOBEO TENNIS COACH AT MIDDLETOWN, N.Y. HIGH SCHOOL, WON 13 CONSECUTIVE CHAMPIONSHIPS, AND HIS PLAYERS *HAVE AN 83-MATCH WINNING STREAK*

THE **STEEPLE** OF THE PALACE IN JOHANNESBURG, SO. AFRICA, THE FIRST 3-STORY BUILDING CONSTRUCTED IN THE CITY, IS MADE *OF CORRUGATED IRON*

A **MAORI** of New Zealand, GREETS A FRIEND BY *STICKING OUT HIS TONGUE*

THE **SCOTCH ARGUS** ON EACH WING HAS THE LETTERS **BO**

A NATURAL ICE BRIDGE
OVER THE VADRET GLACIER
NEAR ALBULA PASS, SWIT.

ALEXANDER FERGUSON
OF DUNDEE, SCOTLAND,
A DOCK MASON, SAVED
55 PERSONS FROM DROWNING-
-ALTHOUGH HE WAS A DEAF-MUTE

DR. JOHN HARVEY KELLOGG
(1852-1943)
FOUNDER OF THE BATTLE CREEK,
MICH., SANITARIUM AND ITS
CHIEF PHYSICIAN FOR 67 YEARS,
ADVOCATED COUNTING CALORIES,
WARNED AGAINST TOBACCO AND
PRAISED YOGURT AND MOLASSES
HALF A CENTURY AGO

LINCKIA COLUMBIAE IS THE ONLY TYPE OF STARFISH THAT CAN GROW A NEW STARFISH *FROM JUST A SMALL PIECE OF AN ARM*

YEZID II

(687-724) 9th CALIPH OF THE MUSLIM EMPIRE, BECAUSE WHITE WAS THE OFFICIAL COLOR OF A RIVAL DYNASTY, ORDERED THE SLAYING OF ALL *WHITE ROOSTERS, WHITE PIGEONS AND WHITE DOGS*

THE SILVER PAVILION of Kyoto, Japan, BUILT IN 1483, *WAS CONSTRUCTED WITHOUT THE USE OF SILVER ··· IT WAS PLANNED TO COVER IT WITH SILVER, BUT IT WAS NEVER DONE*

A **FROG** FOUND BY DAVID LIEBMAN of Norfolk, VA., HAS **14 LEGS**

IN MEMORY OF BEZA WOOD DEPARTED THIS LIFE ~ NOV. 2, 1837 ~ HERE LIES ONE WOOD ENCLOSED IN WOOD, ONE WOOD WITHIN ANOTHER THE OUTER WOOD IS VERY GOOD ~ WE CANNOT PRAISE THE OTHER

EPITAPH – IN WINSLOW, ME.

MEN OF THE TURKANA TRIBE, of Africa, WEAR THE HAIR OF A DECEASED RELATIVE IN AN ELABORATE WOVEN COIFFURE THAT ENDS WITH A LONG WIRE PIGTAIL AND A TUFT OF WOOL

THE MONASTERY OF POTALA IN LHASA, TIBET, IS PAINTED WHITE, RED AND BROWN- *THE SACRED COLORS OF THE TIBETANS*

COWS IN THE VILLAGE OF LA RIERA, SPAIN, AS A PROTECTION AGAINST RAIN AND SUN, WEAR SHEEPSKIN HATS

"HERBIE" A CAT OWNED BY ERROL MAULER OF Bellingham, Wash., OBEYS HALF A DOZEN COMMANDS --*INCLUDING DIALING A TELEPHONE*

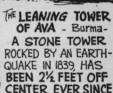

THE **LEANING TOWER OF AVA** - Burma -
A STONE TOWER ROCKED BY AN EARTH-QUAKE IN 1839, HAS BEEN 2½ FEET OFF CENTER EVER SINCE

DEBBIE LAZARZ
OF FARIBAULT, MINN.,
CLAPPED HER HANDS STEADILY FOR 20 HOURS!
Submitted by Bill Schneider, Kerrville, Texas

A **MONUMENT** on Bardsey Island, North Wales, IS A MEMORIAL TO "**20,000** SAINTS" WHOSE ASHES WERE TRANSPORTED THERE WHEN INVADERS DESTROYED A CEMETERY IN Bangor on Dee, England, **1300 YEARS AGO**

DONKEYS' MILK WAS ONCE PEDDLED IN SEGOVIA, SPAIN, AS A CURE FOR *COLDS AND FEVER*

A **HUGE DOORWAY ARCH** IN THE DESERT TOWN OF KHALO BUST, AFGHANISTAN, IS THE ONLY THING REMAINING FROM AN *ANCIENT MOSQUE THAT ONCE OCCUPIED THE SITE*

HENRY WALTER BATES (1825-1892) COLLECTED IN THE AMAZON AREA OF SO. AMERICA 14,700 BUTTERFLIES -- OF *WHICH 8,000 WERE VARIETIES PREVIOUSLY UNKNOWN*

YOUNG SO. **AFRICAN LUNGFISH** ARE GRAY AT NIGHT AND BLACK IN THE DAY-- *CHANGING COLOR TWICE EACH DAY*

THE SUBMARINE BIRD THE GREAT NORTHERN DIVER CAN SWIM UNDERWATER *FOR 10 MINUTES*

THE **FOUR EYE** A FISH OF THE CHAETODON FAMILY, APPEARS TO HAVE AN EXTRA EYE ON EACH SIDE OF ITS BODY

163

SKOGAHOLM MANOR
AN EXHIBIT IN AN OPEN-AIR MUSEUM IN STOCKHOLM, SWEDEN, WAS ORIGINALLY BUILT IN OREBRO, SWEDEN, TAKEN *APART AND SHIPPED 130 MILES TO ITS PRESENT SITE*

GIRLS OF THE LUMBWA TRIBE OF AFRICA, FOR A PERIOD OF 8 MONTHS BEFORE THEY BECOME OLD ENOUGH FOR MARRIAGE, *MUST CONCEAL THEIR FACE AND BODY WITH ANIMAL SKINS*

THE MONASTERY
ON HENGSHAW MOUNTAIN, CHINA, *IS BUILT INTO THE SOLID ROCK AND OVERHANGS A VALLEY FAR BELOW IT*

A KNIFE HANDLE FOUND IN A GRAVE NEAR Andernach, Germany, in 1883, WAS CARVED FROM A REINDEER HORN IN THE LIKENESS OF A SWALLOW 20,000 YEARS AGO.

CARROT THAT GREW THRU A PIECE OF PLASTIC CORD... Submitted by NEIL GILKER, MISSISSAUGA, ONT.

ESKIMOS

IN THE ARCTIC, TO ASSURE RECOVERY OF THEIR HARPOON, ATTACH *A LINE AFFIXED TO AN INFLATED SEALSKIN*

THE CHURCH OF ST. MICHAEL IN ST. SEGIMON, SPAIN, WHICH REQUIRED 200 YEARS TO BUILD, IS NOW *USED AS A STABLE*

THE WATER-TIGER — –AN INSECT– LIVES IN THE WATER BUT BREATHES AIR THROUGH *2 HAIRY SNORKELS*

THE **OBELISK** OF **NUTHURST** ENGLAND, WAS ERECTED IN 1749 BY SIR THOMAS ARCHER TO COMMEMORATE THE JOYFUL MOMENT WHEN HIS WIFE ACCEPTED HIS MARRIAGE PROPOSAL

THE CHAPEL of SANTA CROCE IN CASTELFRANCO EMILIA, ITALY, BECAME AN ARMY BARRACKS IN 1915, A HOTEL 5 YEARS LATER, THEN A PRIVATE HOME, AND IS NOW *A COMMERCIAL BUILDING*

CHINESE OARSMEN OFTEN PROPEL THEIR BOAT STANDING ERECT IN IT AND PUSHING FORWARD *ON OARS CROSSED IN FRONT OF THEM*

166

THE TOWER of the CHURCH OF TONGEREN, BELGIUM -- 190 FT. HIGH -- WAS UNDER CONSTRUCTION FOR 142 YEARS

MARCUS KAVANAGH OF DES MOINES, IOWA, SERVED SUCCESSIVELY AS A JUDGE IN 2 STATES -- *IOWA AND ILLINOIS*

A **BLACKSMITH SHOP** NEAR WÖLFNITZ, AUSTRIA, LOCATED IN A MOUNTAIN CAVE, HAS BEEN SHOEING HORSES *FOR CENTURIES*

WOMEN IN THE AREA OF LAKE VICTORIA, AFRICA, WEAR AN AMULET ON THEIR BACKS--*TO PREVENT EVIL SPIRITS FROM SNEAKING UP ON THEM*

THE MULE EARS BIG BEND REGION, TEXAS, TWIN MOUNTAIN PEAKS THAT LOOK LIKE THE *EARS OF A MULE*

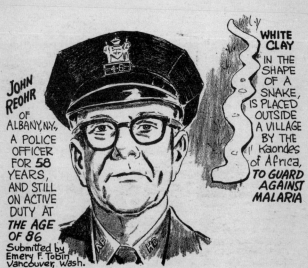

JOHN REOHR OF ALBANY, N.Y., A POLICE OFFICER FOR 58 YEARS, AND STILL ON ACTIVE DUTY AT *THE AGE OF 86* Submitted by Emery F. Tobin Vancouver, Wash.

WHITE CLAY IN THE SHAPE OF A SNAKE, IS PLACED OUTSIDE A VILLAGE BY THE Kaondes of Africa, *TO GUARD AGAINST MALARIA*

168

THE MARBLE YELLOW TEMPLE
IN PEKING, CHINA,
IS A MARBLE TOMB BUILT TO HOLD
*THE CLOTHING OF A GRAND LAMA
OF TIBET WHO DIED OF SMALLPOX.*
THE LAMA'S BODY WAS CARRIED TO
LHASA IN A GOLDEN COFFIN

CANON FREDERICK COOK
(1804-1889) of Exeter, England,
MASTERED 52 LANGUAGES

THE **GATEWAY** TO ROVANIEMI, THE CAPITAL OF FINNISH LAPLAND,
HAS THE NAME OF THE CITY SPELLED OUT IN **REINDEER HORNS**

THE **BONES** OF A **WHALE**
*CONTAIN ALMOST AS MUCH OIL AS CAN BE OBTAINED
FROM ITS BLUBBER* ··· THE BONES ARE SAWED UP AND
BOILED WITH STEAM TO EXTRACT THE OIL

JUNGLE JUICE
Natives of New Guinea, DURING FESTIVALS BUILD A COCKTAIL BAR OUT OF PALM FRONDS, AND SERVE WATI IN COCONUT SHELLS

TOM-TOM DRUMS
USED BY NATIVES OF MALLICOLLO ISLAND IN THE NEW HEBRIDES, ARE CARVED IN THE SHAPE OF *HUMAN FIGURES*

THE PAVILION
OF QUEEN JEANNE, BUILT IN FONTVIEIL, FRANCE, IN THE 14th CENTURY, SO IMPRESSED THE FRENCH POET MISTRAL, THAT BY HIS ORDER A REPLICA WAS ERECTED IN MAILLANE, FRANCE, *AS HIS TOMBSTONE*

CREPIDULA ONYX
A MOLLUSK, GROWS IN BUNCHES OF *AS MANY AS 40*

THE **BRIDGE** OVER THE MAR CANAL IN KASHMIR, INDIA, IS LINED ON EACH *SIDE WITH A ROW OF SHOPS*

BENJAMIN 'FERRIS' FERRARA OF EAST BOSTON, MASS., WEIGHING ONLY 135 LBS., SUPPORTED 4 WOMEN ON A SEE-SAW ON HIS BARE CHEST IN 1926 *WHILE LYING ON SHARP NAILS*

THE **GIMLET GUM** A SMALL AUSTRALIAN TREE, HAS A TRUNK THAT OFTEN IS AS SPIRALLY TWISTED AS A CORKSCREW

THE BARNACLE GOOSE WAS GIVEN THAT NAME BECAUSE OF AN ANCIENT LEGEND THAT GEESE WERE HATCHED FROM *SHIPS' BARNACLES*

THE PAINTING ITS SUBJECT VALUED MORE THAN LIFE!
LORD NELSON FASCINATED BY WEST'S PAINTING OF "THE DEATH OF WOLFE" AND FLATTERED BY THE ARTIST'S PROMISE TO PAINT HIM IN THE SAME MANNER, SAID:
"THEN I HOPE TO DIE IN THE NEXT BATTLE!"
LORD NELSON WAS KILLED IN HIS NEXT BATTLE— AND THE ARTIST KEPT HIS PLEDGE

THE GREAT CATHEDRAL
GORE BAY, NEAR CANTERBURY, N.Z., *NATURAL ROCK FORMATION*

THE GRAVE OF HAMLET HERO OF SHAKESPEARE'S FAMOUS PLAY, IS LOCATED NEAR RANDERS, DENMARK, *BUT HIS REAL NAME WAS AMLED, AND HE WAS A VIKING KING IN THE YEAR 500*

THE ARMY BARRACKS
in Winchester, England,
BUILT IN 1683 AS A ROYAL
PALACE FOR KING CHARLES II,
AND CONVERTED AT THE
MONARCH'S DYING REQUEST
INTO A PRISON,
LATER BECOMING AN
ARMY BARRACKS

MILLET CEREAL
IS ALWAYS
SERVED BY THE
BAFUM TRIBE
of Africa,
IN A WOODEN
DISH CARVED
IN THE FORM
*OF A STATUE
OF THE COOK
WHO INVENTED
THE CEREAL*

**FRANÇOIS-
AUGUSTE de THOU**
(1607-1642)
BECAME GRAND MASTER
OF THE ROYAL LIBRARY
OF PARIS, AND CHIEF
LIBRARIAN OF ALL FRANCE
AT THE AGE OF 10 ...
*25 YEARS LATER HE WAS
EXECUTED FOR TREASON*

ST. STEPHEN
A FISHING
VILLAGE OFF
Montenegro, Yugoslavia,
HAS BEEN CONVERTED
ENTIRELY INTO A
RESORT HOTEL--
*WITH THE OLD
HOMES OF PEASANTS
NOW LUXURY
SUITES*

HALICLYSTUS CYSTA A JELLYFISH, GROWS ON A BLADE OF GRASS -- *FEEDING ON INSECTS WHICH EAT GRASS*

THE **CHURCH GÜNSBACH** in Alsace, France, ALTERNATELY HOLDS CATH-OLIC AND PROTESTANT SERVICES

4-9

LIKE FATHER LIKE SON! John Hay II OF HUON, AUSTRALIA, *MARRIED TWICE AND HAD 22 CHILDREN.*

HIS SON JOHN HAY III *MARRIED TWICE AND ALSO HAD 22 CHILDREN*

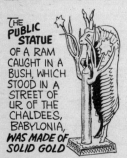

THE **PUBLIC STATUE** OF A RAM CAUGHT IN A BUSH, WHICH STOOD IN A STREET OF UR OF THE CHALDEES, BABYLONIA, *WAS MADE OF SOLID GOLD*

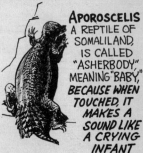

APOROSCELIS A REPTILE OF SOMALILAND, IS CALLED "ASHERBODY," MEANING "BABY," *BECAUSE WHEN TOUCHED, IT MAKES A SOUND LIKE A CRYING INFANT*

THE
**WEATHER
WELL** of
BISEL
Alsace,
France,
BLOWS
OUT AIR
WITH A
LOUD
BLAST TO
FORECAST
*EACH
RAIN-
STORM*

THE HUMAN COMPUTER

JAN ALBERTRANDY (1731-1808)
THE POLISH HISTORIAN,
FORBIDDEN TO COPY HISTORICAL
DOCUMENTS FROM LIBRARIES IN
UPPSALA AND STOCKHOLM, IN SWEDEN,
*MEMORIZED THE ENTIRE CONTENTS
OF 100 VOLUMES—*
HE READ THEM BY DAY IN THE
LIBRARY, AND THEN WROTE DOWN
EVERY WORD AT NIGHT FROM MEMORY
*WITHOUT MAKING A
SINGLE ERROR*

THE **PARISH CHURCH
OF MÜHLDORF
ON THE INN**
Bavaria, HAS BEEN
REBUILT 3 TIMES—
YET ITS ORIGINAL
TOWER IS STILL
STANDING AFTER
743 YEARS

175

AUSTRALIAN ANTS
OBTAIN HONEY
BY TICKLING THE
ABDOMEN OF
LEAFHOPPERS

MRS.
**MOLLIE
REEVES**
OF WAYNE
COUNTY, N.C.,
WHO WAS
BORN IN 1883
IS THE OLDEST *OF 6 LIVING
GENERATIONS IN HER FAMILY*

**YOUNG MAN IN
NATIVE GARB -**
near Gossersweiler,
Germany, NATURAL
ROCK FORMATION

A NEW WIDOW IN A BASQUE HOUSEHOLD,
ACCOMPANIED BY HER OLDEST SON, VISITS THEIR BEEHIVE
TO INFORM THE BEES THAT THEIR MASTER HAS DIED

AN ANCIENT GONG FROM A CHINESE TEMPLE WAS RUNG BY HITTING IT WITH SMALL *BALLS OF COTTON*

FOLLOWERS of the Coconut Monk, on Phoenix Island, WEAR THEIR HAIR SO LONG, IT IS BRAIDED INTO A THICK PIGTAIL AND BALANCED *ON THE WEARER'S HEAD* (South Vietnam)

ALL SAINTS CHURCH at Ainslie, Australia, WAS MOVED 160 MILES TO ITS PRESENT SITE FROM SYDNEY, WHERE IT HAD SERVED FOR NEARLY 100 YEARS **AS A MORTUARY**

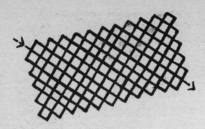

TED ST. MARTIN YAKIMA, WASH. BASKETBALL PLAYER, MADE **927 CONSECUTIVE FREE THROWS** Submitted by Jules H. Marr Albuquerque, N.M.

THE **TONGUE** OF THE DWARF FOUR-TOED SALAMANDER OF GEORGIA *IS MOUNTED ON A STALK GROWING FROM ITS LOWER JAW*

THE CHURCH OF RÄTTVIK - Sweden - IS STILL SURROUNDED BY DOZENS OF WOODEN STABLES IN WHICH PARISH FAMILIES FROM DISTANT HOMES *STABLED THEIR HORSES WHILE ATTENDING SERVICES*

THE MONARCH WHO WAS MUGGED 29 TIMES!

King Kerim Khan (1699-1779) of Persia, SURVIVED 29 ATTACKS AND *PARDONED EVERY ONE OF HIS ASSAILANTS*

A SWEDISH MILE EQUALS 6.2 ENGLISH MILES

3 MI. TO GAS STATION

GAS

THE BELFRY of the Church of Zorge, Germany, IS LOCATED ON A HILL SEVERAL HUNDRED FEET FROM THE CHURCH

Robert OLISLAGERS of ALFRED, N.Y., *TREADED WATER FOR 35 HOURS*

7 SARACEN SKULLS

COLLECTED ON THE BATTLEFIELD OF POITIERS, FRANCE, WHEN CHARLES MARTEL DEFEATED AN INVADING SARACEN HORDE, ARE STILL ON DISPLAY IN A RUINED CHURCH *1,243 YEARS LATER*

THE TOMBSTONES

ON THE GRAVES OF AINU TRIBESMEN ON SACHALIN ISLAND, SOVIET RUSSIA, ARE FORKED STICKS--AND THE LOWER BRANCH INDI-CATES THE POSITION IN WHICH *THE DECEASED WAS BURIED*

A

IN BIERVLIET, NETHERLANDS, ERECTED TO WILLEM BEUKELSZ --FAMED FOR INVENTING A NEW METHOD OF *GUTTING A HERRING*

JANGTANG
A VILLAGE in TIBET, CONSISTS ENTIRELY OF CAVE HOMES *LINKED BY INTERNAL PASSAGES AND STAIRWAYS*

A **CHINESE BANKNOTE**
WORTH ONE AMERICAN CENT--*THE SMALLEST DENOMINATION OF BANKNOTE IN THE WORLD*

THE **BAPTISMAL FONT**
OF THE CHURCH OF Lohja, Finland, A HUGE, 3-TIERED FONT, WAS CARVED *FROM A SINGLE BLOCK OF WOOD*

THE **DECEASED**
IN FUNERALS IN ERIVAN, SOVIET ARMENIA, IS CARRIED TO THE CEMETERY IN AN OPEN CASKET-- WITH THE USUAL FLOWERS *REPLACED BY BUNCHES OF VEGETABLES*

THE $10,000,000 COAT
GRIGORY GRIGORYEVICH ORLOV (1734-1783) A FAVORITE OF RUSSIAN EMPRESS CATHERINE II, WAS PRESENTED BY THE EMPRESS WITH A COAT OF GOLD BROCADE. STUDDED WITH DIAMONDS, FOR WHICH SHE PAID 1,000,000 RUBLES. --*THE EQUIVALENT TODAY OF $10,000,000*

THE AFRICAN WART HOG AS A PRECAUTION AGAINST ATTACK *ALWAYS BACKS INTO ITS BURROW*

HENRY BALDWIN (1780-1844) A JUSTICE OF THE U.S. SUPREME COURT, INVOLVED IN A DUEL AS A YOUTH, ESCAPED DEATH ONLY BECAUSE HIS OPPONENT'S BULLET *LODGED IN A SILVER DOLLAR IN A POCKET IN FRONT OF HIS HEART*

A PELICAN EATS **8 LBS.** OF FISH EACH DAY

A BOOK ABOUT ASBESTOS PRINTED ON ASBESTOS

THE CHURCH of LES VAUXBELETS ON THE ISLE OF GUERNSEY, A REPLICA OF THE CHURCH OF LOURDES, in France, WAS BUILT SINGLE-HANDEDLY BY A MONK *OUT OF COLORFUL BROKEN DISHES*

CRIME DOES PAY IN ALBANIA !
SHAHIN MATARAKU, LEADER OF A BAND OF HIGHWAY ROBBERS in the vicinity of Korča, Albania, *WAS NEVER APPREHENDED ALTHOUGH HE PREYED ON TRAVELERS CONTINUOUSLY FOR 60 YEARS*

THE ROGER SWEETMAN HOUSE in Placentia, Newfoundland, WAS BUILT IN IRELAND IN THE 19th CENTURY, AND TRANSPORTED TO NEWFOUNDLAND *ON ONE OF SWEETMAN'S SHIPS*

DOMESTIC SERVANTS

IN ITALY, BY LAW MUST BE PAID 13 MONTHS' SALARY EACH YEAR -- *THE EXTRA MONTH'S PAY DUE EACH DEC.*

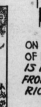

THE TOWER ON THE CITY HALL OF KIRUNA, SWEDEN, *IS MADE OF ORE FROM THE COMMUNITY'S RICH IRON MINE*

ST. SAVIOUR'S ANGLICAN CATHEDRAL in Goulburn, Australia, HAS BEEN UNDER CONSTRUCTION *FOR 90 YEARS*

EMERY F. TOBIN of Vancouver, Wash., IN A PERIOD OF 12 YEARS, HAS HAD MORE THAN **50** SUGGESTIONS PUBLISHED IN **BELIEVE IT OR NOT** !

THE FIRST PAPER MONEY WAS ISSUED IN CHINA IN 650, AND WAS REDEEMABLE IN *TEA OR RICE*

A **LOBSTER** HAS ITS ORGAN OF BALANCE *IN ITS TAIL*

THE **FRA FRA TRIBE** of the African Gold Coast, IS STILL KNOWN BY THAT NAME –GIVEN IT BECAUSE TRIBESMEN GREETED THE FIRST WHITE MEN WITH THE WORDS *"FRA FRA"* – MEANING *"HELLO"*

ALL SAINTS CHURCH in Kilembe, Uganda, *IS ROOFED WITH PAPYRUS*

THIS **MONUMENT** IN LONDON, ENGLAND, HONORING THE DUKE OF YORK, SON OF KING GEORGE III, WAS FINANCED IN 1833 BY WITHHOLDING *THE PAY OF EACH BRITISH SOLDIER FOR ONE DAY*

A **TEMPLE** ON THE YANGTZE RIVER, IN CHINA, WITH A **PORCELAIN FAÇADE**

A **BATCH OF SUNFLOWERS** ALL 10 TO 12 FEET TALL Grown by Aina Anderson, Ravena, N.Y.

PATRICIA LEITH OF LEESBURG VA. CAN PUT HER ***ENTIRE FIST IN HER MOUTH*** Submitted by Sherry Kirk, Leesburg

THE FIRST BICYCLE A STAINED GLASS WINDOW IN STOKE POGES, ENGLAND, DEPICTING A WINGLESS ANGEL ON A "BICYCLE," WAS CREATED IN THE 17th CENTURY ***--NEARLY 200 YEARS BEFORE THE INVENTION OF THE BICYCLE***

A **CHAIR** MADE FROM A RUM CASK, WAS USED BY THE CAPTAIN OF THE AUSTRALIAN BARK "WILD WAVE," TO *SMUGGLE RUM INTO MANY COUNTRIES*

A **TREE** IN VIENNA, AUSTRIA, ON WHICH WREATHS ARE HUNG IN MEMORY OF *VICTIMS OF A STREETCAR ACCIDENT THAT OCCURRED NEARBY*

THE **GROOM** and **BRIDE** IN THE CHAAMBA TRIBE OF THE ALGERIAN SAHARA, MEET FOR THE FIRST TIME AFTER THEY HAVE BEEN MARRIED--AND THE GROOM MUST SLAP HIS WIFE'S FACE 7 TIMES. AT THE SAME TIME EACH SPEAKS THE OTHER'S NAME FOR THE FIRST AND ONLY TIME IN THEIR LIFETIMES

THE OLDEST STONE STRUCTURE IN THE WORLD THE **STEP PYRAMID** of Saqqara, Egypt, WAS CONSTRUCTED **5,000** YEARS AGO

ST. HUBERT'S HUNTING LODGE NOW NETHERLANDS' NATL. PARK, WAS BUILT IN THE SHAPE *OF THE ANTLERS OF A STAG*

THE **FEMALE ARGONAUT** IS 20 TIMES AS LARGE AS THE MALE-- *THE* COMPARATIVE SIZES OF A PEA AND A FOOTBALL

A **WITCH DOCTOR** in Angola, Africa TO RESIGN HIS PROFESSION MUST ATTAIN AN ENTIRELY NEW IDENTITY BY *WEARING A MASK DAY AND NIGHT FOR A WHOLE YEAR*

SEDGWICK

THE **FOUNTAIN of DENT** in England, A MEMORIAL TO GEOLOGIST ADAM SEDGWICK, A NATIVE SON WHO DISCOVERED SHAP GRANITE, *CONSISTS OF A ROUGH BLOCK OF THAT STONE*

EMPEROR ZENO
RULER OF BYZANTIUM FROM 474 TO 491,
WAS BURIED ALIVE!
EMPEROR ANASTASIUS, HIS
SUCCESSOR, LOCKED HIM
IN A MAUSOLEUM
AND HE STARVED TO DEATH

from an old print

DUKAGJINI WOMEN
OF ALBANIA,
REVEAL THEY ARE MARRIED
*BY WEARING HEAVY LEATHER
BELTS 6 INCHES WIDE AND
STITCHED WITH SILVER WIRE*

FUR FLOATS
NATIVES OF THE
NORTHERN COAST OF
CHILE, MAKE
INFLATABLE FLOATS
COMPRISED OF 2
"CYLINDERS" FASHIONED
FROM SEALSKINS

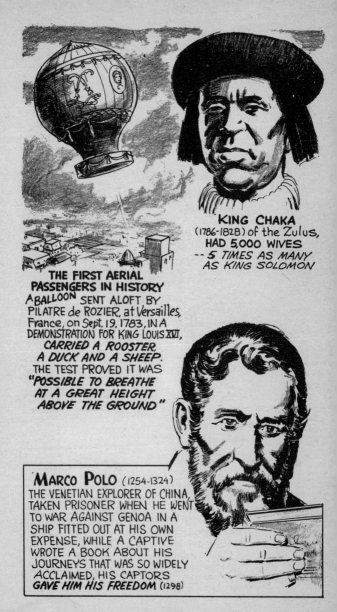

KING CHAKA (1786-1828) of the Zulus, HAD 5,000 WIVES -- 5 TIMES AS MANY AS KING SOLOMON

THE FIRST AERIAL PASSENGERS IN HISTORY A BALLOON SENT ALOFT BY PILATRE de ROZIER, at Versailles, France, on Sept. 19, 1783, IN A DEMONSTRATION FOR KING LOUIS XVI, *CARRIED A ROOSTER, A DUCK AND A SHEEP.* THE TEST PROVED IT WAS *"POSSIBLE TO BREATHE AT A GREAT HEIGHT ABOVE THE GROUND"*

MARCO POLO (1254-1324) THE VENETIAN EXPLORER OF CHINA, TAKEN PRISONER WHEN HE WENT TO WAR AGAINST GENOA IN A SHIP FITTED OUT AT HIS OWN EXPENSE, WHILE A CAPTIVE WROTE A BOOK ABOUT HIS JOURNEYS THAT WAS SO WIDELY ACCLAIMED, HIS CAPTORS *GAVE HIM HIS FREEDOM* (1298)

190

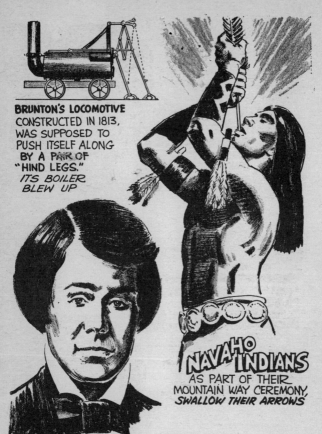

BRUNTON'S LOCOMOTIVE CONSTRUCTED IN 1813, WAS SUPPOSED TO PUSH ITSELF ALONG BY A PAIR OF "HIND LEGS." *ITS BOILER BLEW UP*

NAVAHO INDIANS AS PART OF THEIR MOUNTAIN WAY CEREMONY, *SWALLOW THEIR ARROWS!*

BRIGADIER GENERAL THOMAS L. HAMER AS A CONGRESSMAN FROM OHIO, APPOINTED ULYSSES S. GRANT TO WEST POINT *UNDER THE WRONG NAME!* GRANT'S NAME ACTUALLY WAS HIRAM ULYSSES GRANT, BUT HE HAD TO ADOPT THE NAME UNDER WHICH HAMER HAD MISTAKENLY APPOINTED HIM A CADET

THE **POST** ON A STREET CORNER IN Rostock, Germany, IS THE BARREL OF AN ANCIENT CANNON

Sandy ALLEN of Shelbyville, Indiana, AT THE AGE OF 19 WEIGHS **421 POUNDS**, WEARS A SIZE **16 EEE** SHOE AND IS **7 FEET, 5½ INCHES TALL**

THE **FLOWING CHASM OF THINGVELLIR** Iceland, CONTAINS THOUSANDS OF COINS DROPPED IN THE BELIEF THE SACRIFICE *WILL BRING GOOD FORTUNE*

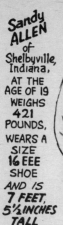

A **HEART-SHAPED BOOK** MADE IN 1590 FOR THE WIFE OF THE RULER OF SAXONY, CONTAINED *SUGGESTIONS FOR* **DOMESTIC ECONOMIES**

ACANTHARIA A MARINE PROTOZOAN KNOWN AS A RADIOLARIAN, HAS A SKELETON COMPOSED OF STRONTIUM SULPHATE-- *AN ELEMENT SO RARE IN OCEAN WATER THAT SCIENTISTS CAN FIND ONLY MINUTE TRACES OF IT*

THE **PELICAN'S BEAK** DOES INDEED *"HOLD MORE THAN ITS BELLY CAN."* ITS BEAK HAS A CAPACITY OF MORE THAN **25 POUNDS** OF FISH